The
SONG in YOU

Finding Your Voice,
Redefining Your Life

LaDonna Gatlin, CSP, CPAE and
Mike Marino, PhD

Health Communications, Inc.
Deerfield Beach, Florida

www.hcibooks.com

Bible quotations throughout the book are taken from the New International Version unless otherwise noted.

Photos on page 258 are used with permission: (clockwise from top)

©1955 Gatlin family photo
©1960 Gatlin family photo
©2005 Photographybydov.com
©2006 Gatlin family photo
©2011 Don Sparks Photography
©2011 Don Sparks Photography
©1974 Benjamin Photography

Library of Congress Cataloging-in-Publication Data

Gatlin, LaDonna.
   The song in you : finding your voice, redefining your life / LaDonna Gatlin and Mike Marino.
     p. cm.
   ISBN 978-0-7573-1622-7 (trade paper)
   ISBN 0-7573-1622-0 (trade paper)
   ISBN 978-0-7573-1623-4 (epub)
   ISBN 0-7573-1623-9 (epub)
    1. Conduct of life.   2. Self-realization.   3. Gatlin, LaDonna.   I. Marino, Mike, PhD.
  II. Title.
   BJ1589.G38 2012
   158.1—dc23

                                      2012018082

©2012 LaDonna Gatlin and Mike Marino

Publisher: Health Communications, Inc.
          3201 S.W. 15th Street
          Deerfield Beach, FL 33442–8190

Cover image by: ConstanceAshley.com
Cover and interior design by Lawna Patterson Oldfield

CONTENTS

FOREWORD

Sis,

Where do I start? I know when writing a foreword to a book it's customary to address it to the folks who are holding the book somewhere in a bookstore (are there any bookstores left?) or have bought the book and are just sitting down in their cozy chairs to begin reading it. And I know that I'm supposed to tell the above-mentioned cozy-chair-sittin' readers just what I think of the author and the book.

Well, sis, you know I ain't normal, and you know I don't usually do things the way everybody else does . . . and thank God most have cut me some slack in that regard! You see, sis, at sixty-three years old, with the road ahead a whole lot shorter than the road behind, I figure it's high time I tell you how I feel about you.

Simply put, you are the berries—best sister, daughter, wife, mother, grandmother, or friend a person could ever have! Kind of a homely old gal, but with a real good personality (just kiddin'). In truth, you are beautiful, inside and out, and you have a generous heart and a giving spirit. You are a great speaker and motivator, funny, and truth be told— and I will tell the truth—you are the best singer in the whole dad-burned Gatlin family! It kinda galls me to have to say it, and you know it galls the other two (you know who) too! And now on top of all of that, you are an author—and a dad- burned good one! Congrats!! Sis, Larry loves ya and is proud of ya . . . and if the "cozy-chair sitters" don't like the book, well they ain't got no taste, couth, or sense.

Keep the faith,
Larry

Chapter 1

GROWING UP GATLIN

ABILENE, TEXAS, AUGUST 18, 1954. On their fourth try, Billie and Curley Gatlin *finally* welcomed a daughter into the Gatlin family! I was just fifteen minutes into this world when Dad tied a pink ribbon in my hair and anointed me family "princess"! My brothers, Larry, Steve, and Rudy, already performing veterans at ages six, four, and two, respectively, were *crazy* about me!

Crazy might be a good word to describe the path my life has taken . . . from the highest highs of show business to an overwhelming war with sadness that led me to try to take my own life. Some have described me as a resilient Texas toughie who survived and eventually thrived in sometimes difficult personal and professional circumstances, but I see it a little differently.

I've learned that my life, in fact life in general, has good parts and bad parts. They simply coexist. Embracing that truth has opened the door for more honest and authentic living, and that's really what this book is about—accepting and enthusiastically embracing what is. My hope is that after reading the book you'll find the special and unique song in you, and that as you discover your own voice, you'll live with refreshed purpose and passion.

My journey toward honest and authentic living has had more than a few bumps along the way. Drawing the line between reality and make-believe is a dilemma for many of us in show business. Even as a young child I learned that true "professionals" put on their "happy face" and best effort when the stage lights come on. The old adage "the show must go on" was, and still is, in my DNA.

Don't get me wrong, I *love* performing. Speaking and singing is how I've made my living for many years. The spotlight is truly a happy place for me, but drawing the line between where the performance stops and real life begins can be confusing. It has caused me problems, and as the worldwide press and tabloids have often reported, it's been a struggle for my famous brothers as well.

It all started with the music. When my mom was just a girl, it was common practice for her dad, "Papa Doan," to pack up the family and head out to all-day "Gospel Singings." He repeatedly challenged her to learn everything she could about music and not be afraid to take a risk and try something new. "I'd rather sing a new song badly than an old one well," he'd say.

(What a great metaphor for life, by the way!) That philosophy was passed on to us by my mother.

Looking back, I think this musical risk-taking attitude shaped much of what lay ahead for the Gatlins, especially Larry. As we blossomed into our careers, our trademark Gatlin family harmony and Larry's beautifully penned lyrics and melodies hit Nashville and the country music scene like a fresh wind—one that drew fans and followers from across the musi cal spectrum. As country music surged into the mainstream, my big brother was among those leading the charge. I was, and am, so very proud of all my brothers. My life's view will always be colored with shades of love and respect for Larry, Steve, and Rudy.

When I was three years old, we moved to Odessa, Texas. West Texas in 1957 was everything you might imagine—tough men who worked in the oilfields, churchgoing women, and the pre–health food, grease-filled burger joint, Nicky's Drive-In—where you might spot young Roy Orbison looking for a *Pretty Woman* (yes, he really lived nearby and was a fixture on the local teen scene).

Our childhood was filled with an odd mix of simple-to-understand truths and complicated ambition. In some ways life still feels that way today. Of course, we had no cell phones, Internet, or terrorist threats in West Texas. Right was right, wrong was wrong, and, at least in West Texas, men were men. It felt pretty safe having an ex-marine dad and three heroic older brothers to protect and nurture me. Still, being the only (sibling) girl in a family that lived, sang, and performed together had certain drawbacks. Any traveling music group with girls involved will invariably confront some of the age-old male-female struggles: *She brings too much luggage. What takes her so long to get ready? Why do we have to stop for so many potty breaks?* and so on.

As idyllic as West Texas was in America's *Happy Days* era, the Gatlin Quartet (I had now officially joined my brothers) was often too busy to enjoy lazy weekends and summer days. Our signature four-part harmony seemed to be a hit wherever we performed. Being onstage and singing just felt natural to us. On some level we thought this was what normal kids did with their free time, although the boys still made time for sports and girls (more about that later . . .). Whatever, wherever, whenever, we'd suit up, show up, and sing our little heads off. From the county fair to the world's fair (literally), we blew our audiences away! And we began to learn that there were tangible benefits to show business. Once we took first prize in a local talent show and won a Shetland pony! Actually, I would have preferred the second prize, a Chinese dinner at a local restaurant—now that sounded like a great adventure!

In that simpler time, traveling the country and receiving thunderous accolades was a pretty heady thing for the young Gatlin Quartet. We got to meet the famous, almost-famous, and soon-to-be famous . . . and you can imagine the wide-eyed wonderment on our faces as we drove into New York City! Incredibly, through Mom's bulldog tenacity, we got to perform at the 1964 World's Fair! Wow! From oil-soaked Odessa, Texas, to the Big Apple. This was not the county fair—this was the *world's* fair! Of course, as a kid it's really hard to capture the true scope of an event and performing opportunity like that. In the midst of this international showcase for new technology, diversity, and ideology, I just wanted a snow cone! Already the cool, calm professional, I took it in stride as just another stop along our path to stardom. Of course, I always felt safe and confident, knowing my mom and brothers were there to lean on—especially Larry.

I really can't say enough good things about Larry's talent, creativity, and dogged determination. In those days you could get your driver's permit at age fourteen in Texas, and he became Mom's relief driver on our many cross-country journeys. Our dad stayed at home, working most of the time; somebody had to help fund our early musical endeavors! So Larry became the "on-the-road patriarch" by default. Larry was our "go-to" guy. What a hero—handsome, great singer, football star, and a man's man (as much as a fourteen-year-old can be!).

As you might imagine, Mom had her hands full traveling with four of us. We were typical kids; we didn't always get along. Sometimes, due to simple logistics, we would barely make it to a performance. One thing for sure though, when we got on stage, we sounded, looked, and acted the part of the most well-mannered, polished professionals you've ever seen. No one would have ever imagined the hectic wardrobe change that had taken place in the back of the station wagon just minutes before.

Our mom was the ultimate "stage mom," and I mean that in the most flattering sense. She always made sure we were taken care of: our little matching suits cleaned and pressed, our hair neatly combed, and our shoes shined. Dad was our strict, marine-style disciplinarian, but Mom was all heart. And that combination worked; we needed both. We learned our "never give up" work ethic from him, and Mom's encouragement planted the seeds that nourished our blossoming talent. From a developmental perspective, psychologists tell us that kids need their moms most when they're little and growing into adolescence. I'm convinced the unconditional love we received from Mom allowed us to develop the self-confidence to explore our God-given, creative passions.

Through our teen years, we began to discover our own paths. I was into everything fun at high school: pep squad, sports, good girlfriends, and, yes, I had the teenage hormone thing working as well. Boys were on my mind!

Larry won a football scholarship to the University of Houston, where he caught a touchdown pass in a record-setting 100–6 victory over the University of Tulsa! Steve and Rudy soon followed Larry into college, but our hearts never drifted far from the music.

Of course, we still led dual lives as acclaimed performers on the weekends and during summer vacation. It really was kind of a weird "double life." We were just normal kids who got standing ovations for our singing on the weekends and slept through geometry during the week. I guess we were the gospel version of TV's *Partridge Family*. Looking back I can see how much our parents sacrificed to feed our creative talents while keeping a sense of normalcy for us; our heads were in the clouds, but our feet were on the ground. Thank you, Mom and Dad!

Still, it remained crystal clear that there was a musical calling on this family, one that would prove to be a double-edged sword in the years to come. One of the great myths of the country music world, and even the gospel music world, is that these genres are somehow inherently more wholesome than other musical communities, like jazz, rock, or pop. Fame and fortune brought mixed blessings to the Gatlin family—super-high peaks and deep, dark valleys.

Success often takes the most unlikely turns. One thing for sure, we Gatlins were going to be prepared should our big opportunity arise. That's exactly what happened for Larry. While in college Larry was asked to join the celebrated gospel quartet the Imperials, who were appearing with country music star Jimmy Dean in Las Vegas. Larry jumped at the chance and, predictably, "blew their socks off." He soon found himself moving to Nashville and writing songs for the industry megastars of that day. Music legend Dottie West became Larry's biggest fan. He wrote for her publishing company, and she introduced him to the A-list of country music. Soon it seemed like everyone was recording a Larry Gatlin song: Kris Kristofferson, Johnny Cash, even Elvis!

While Larry was lighting up the Nashville music scene, I kept my musical dreams moving as well. While I was attending Odessa Junior College in 1974, one of our childhood musical hero groups, the Blackwood Singers, called and asked me to join them for their summer tour. My parents were against it, but I turned on the "princess" charm and convinced them—it would be a decision that shaped my life forever! It turned out they also needed a piano player, and their producer, Phil Johnson, called his brother Tim and said, "Tim, I've got a job and a girl for you!" Thirty-seven years later Tim and I are still married. Thank God, I've had the rock of my relationship with

Tim to cling to for all these years. As both Tim and I were about to discover, things can get really funky on the road with a big-time star.

Anyone who remotely followed music in the 1960s and 1970s knew the name Tammy Wynette. Her pop-country smash hit "Stand by Your Man" rang as an anthem of fidelity for generations of women who weren't too sure about the then-burgeoning feminist movement. Tammy had recorded one of Larry's songs, and he learned that she was looking for a backup vocal group to tour with. Big brother Larry arranged for us to meet her at her palatial Nashville home. So, with the confidence of youth and years of experience on my side, I walked into her home, along with my new husband, Tim, and brother Rudy, to meet her.

I thought we were just going to meet, but she had us audition right then and there. To use a show business term—we *killed* her! We were hired on the spot for her upcoming tour, and our brother Steve soon joined us as we performed in the Tammy Wynette show under the name of Young Country.

For the next fourteen months we played the biggest venues in the biggest cities of the world. Oh, the sights we saw and the great fun we had! But as has been well documented in show business history, boredom and monotonous routine often cause free-spirited touring musicians to seek release from the long hours of travel and waiting to perform. Tim and I just weren't comfortable with some of what we saw, and as the tabloid newspapers quickly exposed, brother Rudy and Tammy were becoming more than just friends. The situation got increasingly tense with the press printing graphic and hurtful stories about Rudy and Tammy, and Tim and I were doing anything we could to stay above the drama. Thankfully, as things began to fall apart with the Tammy Wynette tour, Larry came to the rescue!

Even though his record label, Monument, wanted him as a solo act, Larry had a different plan in mind. In the years that followed, music industry executives would come to learn that Larry is very particular about his music. He knows what he wants—and he wanted us! Frankly, Larry could have hired any musicians in Nashville, but he flatly told his producers, "No. I want my family here, and we'll be called Larry Gatlin—with Family and Friends." My hero! He brought the family back together to sing again!

As Larry's first big Gatlin hit "Broken Lady" was being released, we began to do isolated performing dates and showcases. There wasn't a lot of work, but we were together and could see that good things were ahead. Still, I just hated it that we'd play in small venues where "overserved patrons" would heckle us, especially when Larry took the stage solo with just his guitar. If you know anything about Larry, you know that he is not one to let a drunken catcall go. Larry is one of those rare talents who can hold a crowd captivated with just his voice and guitar. He can move them from laughter to tears in a matter of moments, and watching him was like going to school. As my life took a different path and I became a motivational and inspirational speaker, I've often reflected on what I learned just watching my big brother. I can trace many of the subtle inflections I use back to what I learned in those formative years.

However, the helpful education I was receiving was something of a two-sided coin. Many of the things Tim and I saw behind the scenes really clarified our perspective on the less-attractive side of the music business. The infidelity, drugs, and booze, and the lack of integrity in "showbiz," put a little damper on our enthusiasm. Of course, we had no idea what life-changing events were about to unfold. Our world was about to change forever.

The film *The Cross and the Switchblade* made quite a splash when it was released in 1970. It was the true story of the relationship between Christian evangelist David Wilkerson (played by Pat Boone) and New York gang leader Nicky Cruz (played by Erik Estrada). Buoyed by the hit movie, David Wilkerson expanded his worldwide series of evangelistic crusades to tell his story. Feeling he needed music to set the framework for these events, he asked recording artist Dallas Holm, who was then making his mark in the new field of contemporary Christian music, to join him.

My brother-in-law Phil was again to play a pivotal role in our lives. He was producing Dallas Holm's records at that time, and Dallas wanted to put a band together. He called Phil to see if he knew anyone who might be interested. Knowing we were struggling with the Nashville music scene, Phil recommended us for the crusade tours. Talk about Divine intervention! We flew to Wilkerson's Texas headquarters and the rest, as they say, is history. Dallas had just written the now-classic song "Rise Again." As he began to sing it, Tim and I joined him on the chorus. It was a God moment. It became obvious that this was meant to be, and we were offered the job. The group Dallas Holm and Praise was born.

We flew back to Nashville and the hard reality set it. Larry Gatlin with Family and Friends had a hit record on the way with "Broken Lady"; how could we tell him, Steve, and Rudy we wanted to leave the family group when fame and fortune finally seemed within our grasp? We had a tough decision to make. After much thought and prayer in our circa 1970s olive-green carpeted Nashville apartment (can you believe we thought that was hip?), Tim and I decided to tell Larry we felt called to leave the family group. To say that didn't go over well would be quite an understatement! It caused disconnection and pain in our family for years to come. Larry does not like to hear the word "no"—especially from his little sis.

I can certainly understand his reaction. Was this really God's call on our lives or just a noble escape from country music? In retrospect it seems pretty clear that this was the path for Tim and me to pursue God's plan and purpose for our lives. At the time, who can say for sure? I am sometimes suspicious when people tell me they're certain they've heard from God. It's not that I don't believe God can influence our thoughts and actions. We have the Bible, we have other people of faith who can very often be a tangible reflection of God's love and character, and we have the still, small voice inside (some call it our conscience) that seems to intuitively know the right choice. Still, at the end of the day, I think we're left with the free will to choose, and we don't always get it right. This time I think we did. I believe even Larry would agree with that today.

Now when I speak and sing, I often reflect on the hard decision Tim and I had before us back then. Much of this book centers on the premise that making good decisions opens the door for ultimate fulfillment. We all face choices in life, and I believe choices are one of the very few things in our control. In truth, we don't control the outcome of events, only our actions along the way. I've found that sometimes making the difficult, but right choice can bring peace and fulfillment beyond the temporary results (much more on that in Chapter 2).

At first things weren't so clear, but soon it became obvious we'd made the right choice. Just as Tim and I made the move to Texas, Larry, Steve, and Rudy began to hit the showbiz stratosphere. If we hadn't gotten out when we did, I don't think we ever would have. Larry won a Grammy Award that year for writing "Broken Lady." It would have been too hard to leave after that, and we might have missed the different path God had us on. With my voice missing from the family group, Rudy began to sing the high harmony part, and their three-part harmony evolved into the signature "Gatlin Brothers sound" that sustained them through multiple hit records—and still fills concert halls today! In the long run, it's worked out best for all of us.

While my brothers were doing their thing, Tim and I were doing ours. Dallas Holm and Praise recorded their first record in 1976 in a high school auditorium in Lindale, Texas. It became one of the first albums in contemporary Christian music to earn a gold record. We crisscrossed the country with the Wilkerson crusades, and as you can imagine, the last thing on our minds was starting a family. But you guessed it—surprise! I got pregnant! I stayed on the road until the guys got tired of hearing me throw up on the bus (the joys of pregnancy!). Tim continued to tour with the group, but I went back to Lindale and had a little production of my own: our son Caleb was born in 1978.

So that's the way it went. Tim traveled playing music and I stayed home being a mom and a baby factory. In 1981 our second child, Annie, came along. My brothers were rocketing to the highest orbit of the show business galaxy, and I was changing diapers. As fulfilling as being a mom was, I missed performing. Sure, I'd do an occasional church event, but inside I felt a stirring to explore a new path, to sing a new song. That spark ignited a passion that became my transformation from "former Gatlin" to Hall of Fame motivational speaker: a fresh chapter in my life and a new song to sing—what a ride! You may be reading this thinking, *I used to be "that" and could never become "this."* You are not alone. Over the years countless people have come up to me after my speaking engagements to share how they've lost hope. I tell them—and I'm telling you— things can change, and I am living proof. And if you finish reading this book, you'll have some proven tools to get movin' with the rest of your life!

As I began my transition to a professional speaker (I still sing as part of my presentations), I observed that while I had an aptitude for this, I still had much to learn. At the same time, it was exciting and uncomfortable. I am a seasoned performer, but holding a crowd's attention and emotions with just words?

That's a whole different ball game. One thing that did feel eerily familiar from my days on the big music stage was that you never really know who is in the audience or how just one night might change your life.

At an event in a small Baptist church, a very successful motivational speaker named Andy Hickman was in the audience. He approached me and asked, "How would you like to take your message outside the church walls?" I was very cautious; this seemed like a 180-degree turn from where I'd been as a performer, wife, and mother. But Andy persisted and introduced me to the right people. At forty-two I began to reinvent my life, and by 2005 I was inducted into the National Speakers Association Hall of Fame! Never in my wildest imagination did I think this was a possibility. I'm just a country gal from Texas, and today I routinely speak to corporations, associations, educators, faith-based groups, and countless industry leaders from all over the country. This plan, I believe God's plan for my life, wasn't even on the radar when Tim and I broke the news to the family that we were going to follow a different path. Their path was their path, mine is mine. What about yours?

Of course, it hasn't all been fun. Through my personal metamorphosis Tim and I have lived through some scary times. Just after Annie was born, Tim was diagnosed with cancer. Cancer—who plans for that? This was a great lesson for us. We embraced a truth that I think most of know down deep but rarely want to look at. The truth is life does not revolve around our wishes or timetable. Sometimes stuff just happens and you deal with it.

While Tim responded well to treatment, his cancer ultimately resurfaced in 2009. Thankfully, cancer is not the death sentence it was a generation ago, and Tim is doing well. A year earlier, in 2008, when I attended the National Speakers Association convention, their theme was *NSA Rocks!* The convention was filled with cutting-edge technology and a new generation of "thirty-something" speakers. I kept thinking, *I'm fifty-four years old, and I don't rock! All of this technology and youth is passing me by!* Maybe I overreacted, but concerns about Tim's health and my future as a speaker began to overwhelm me.

I wasn't eating; I was losing weight, not sleeping, and felt like I was careening into a black hole of hopelessness. Looking back I can see the clear signals that clinical depression was staking its claim in my mind, body, and spirit. Depression runs in my family. I guess I shouldn't have been surprised, but who thinks practically or clearly in the midst of that battle? Like most performers, I was able to rise to the occasion when working (the show must go on!), but behind the scenes, I slept all day and downed prescription tranquilizers and antidepressants just to function.

Wednesday, November 19, 2008. This was the day I nearly stepped into eternity, leaving behind any hope for fulfilling my earthly purpose. This was the day my husband, children, brothers, and parents may have marked as our last together.

Here's the crazy part: I really don't even remember how it happened. All I know is that I woke up in the emergency room after taking handfuls of pills. As I stared up into the faces of Tim, our pastor, Annie, and her husband, my first instinct was to minimize the incident as an accident. I've since learned this is a common coping mechanism for people who attempt suicide. No one was buying it. To put it in Southern vernacular, "That dog wouldn't hunt"—and soon I found myself walking through the doors of a locked inpatient psychiatric hospital.

Depression is an insidious and often silent killer. Dr. Mike Marino, my cowriter (God bless him!), is an expert on the subject and has written books about it. In the hospital I learned that I was not alone. We average more than thirty thousand deaths from suicide each year in the United States. That's twice the number of homicides! And for every successful suicide attempt, there are at least eight failed attempts like mine. Many never even get reported. Depression and suicide are big problems.

In the psychiatric hospital I began to wonder if my speaking career was over. After all, who is interested in life advice from someone who reached a point where she couldn't handle her own? But with God's help and typical Gatlin stubbornness, I was determined to move toward wellness and step way out on a limb. I began to tell this difficult part of my story at my speaking engagements. I knew this could not be something I hid in the closet, but rather I had to tell it for my own sake if for no one else's. I've discovered there's genuine healing power in naming your struggles. Accurately identifying what they are and where they may have come from seems to take away their power. Still, as I began to share my depression and suicide story in public, I was gripped by a terror that screamed this might be the end of my speaking livelihood.

I could not have been more wrong. People are more than just accepting of my story—they embrace it. While their personal struggles may have different shades, I've learned that everyone deals with their portion of pain. While it is not the sum of our life experience, trouble is an unavoidable part of it. Many times people say they feel like I "get" them and understand what struggle is about. *Wow,* I think, *what an honor to make them feel heard and understood!* I think we all want that, and in the pages of this book, I hope you'll feel like I "get" at least a part of you.

As I travel the country, one of the real pleasures is that I get to meet and connect with so many interesting people. Sometimes I feel like the actress Sally Field, who said in her now-famous Academy Award acceptance speech, "You like me; you really like me!" I had been afraid of losing my audience to the youthful, high-tech boom, but I discovered that sharing my entire story, the highs *and* the lows, resonates with everyone. A whole new message and following has opened for me.

I've discovered that it is never too late to make a positive change. I've seen it in my life and the life of my family. For example, apart from what his songs did for others, Larry and the Gatlin Brothers hit number one on the charts three times and scored an astonishing thirty-three top-forty hits! However, as he shares publicly, in the early 1980s Larry was crawling on a Dallas hotel room floor, snorting up pieces of lint in hopes they were cocaine. He'd been up for days in a drug-induced haze and finally made his way to the mirror. As he looked at the shadow of a human in the reflection, he hit his personal bottom and committed to recovery. Things can change! People can change! While Larry still performs with the brothers today, he also has reinvented himself as a social commentator, sitting in as host of the nationally syndicated Don Imus radio program and as a frequent guest on various programs on the Fox News Network. If you find yourself in a bad spot today, I want to encourage you: your circumstances can change and you are not finished. I know what hopelessness feels like, but my life story is proof that there is life beyond the storm.

I want everyone who reads this book and hears my message to embrace their God-given potential, redeem their precious time, and find a future in their failures, just as my brothers and I have. Back in 1960s West Texas, I'm not sure anyone would have imagined those Gatlin kids would ever amount to much. I mean, really, we hadn't even heard of the *National Enquirer*—who knew we'd wind up in it! There's no way we'd stay together as a family after all the struggles we had personally and as a group. There's no way I could transition from a singer and diaper-changing mom to a Hall of Fame speaker. And there's certainly no way I could climb out of that psychiatric bed to return to inspire and motivate hundreds of thousands nationwide.

But I did! And you can find rich meaning and purpose in *your* life as well!

Chapter 2

DO:
Do the
Right Thing

F ROM THE TIME I WAS just a little girl, I knew I wanted to stand on a stage with a microphone and sing to people. I sensed music and carefully chosen words could truly speak to people—and potentially change their lives. With all the unfettered zeal of youth, I envisioned my music inspiring others to become all God created them to be. I knew this was possible because someone did it for me, and I will never forget the day it happened.

It was the summer of 1965, and I was eleven years old. I'll save you the trouble of doing the math. Depending on when you read this book, I'm older than fifty, but not yet ready for the senior home! The summer of '65 was a scorcher in West Texas, with record-breaking heat waves and not nearly enough trips to Nicky's Drive-In for an ice-cream treat. One sweltering Sunday afternoon, my mom popped her head into my bedroom and said, "Hey, LaDonna, I have a great idea—let's go to the movies." I thought that was a brilliant idea because, in addition to a fun afternoon of entertainment, the movie theater had air-conditioning. That was a big, big (did I mention *big*?) deal in the West Texas triple-digit heat of that summer.

We hopped into the car and away we went. As if it were yesterday, I remember our arrival at that theater with the same giddy expectation. It's funny how things always seem bigger and grander when you're a kid. Still, even with all my hopeful expectation for a little cool refreshment and some tasty treats, I couldn't have even imagined how that day would change my life. My mother plopped down a ten dollar bill at the ticket window—good for two tickets to the Sunday afternoon matinee, two popcorns, two large Peanut M&M'S, and two jumbo Cokes—and my mother even got back some change! (Note to readers: this was a *long* time ago!)

We walked into that wonderfully air-conditioned theater and sat down right in the middle. As we settled into our seats, the lights dimmed, those big black velvet curtains opened up, and there she was on that hillside, with her arms all flung out singing, "The hills are alive with the sound of music." I was captivated! I sat up on the edge of my seat and, I swear, my eyes bugged out. My mouth flew open, and I thought, *Man, this lady can sing!* Of course, the movie was the now-classic *The Sound of Music*, and I drank in every moment. But as the story unfolded, it wasn't just the music that made an impact on me. It was the way Julie Andrews so beautifully portrayed the life of Maria von Trapp. It was the way she lived her life that made an indelible impression on my eleven-year-old heart, mind, and soul.

As the story progressed, Maria became the governess for the seven von Trapp children and taught them a variety of life lessons and skills, including singing. Even though the movie "had" me from the opening credits, the singing part drew me in with a gut-shaking fascination. She taught the children to sing using a method known as solfège, or more commonly known to us as "do, re, mi, fa, sol, la, ti, do."

Solfège really represents the very basics or the absolute essentials of music. If you look up the term *solfège* in a music dictionary, it is defined as "a technique for the teaching of sight-singing in which each note of the score is sung to a special syllable, called a solfège syllable. The seven syllables commonly used for this practice in English-speaking countries are: do, re, mi, fa, sol, la, and ti, which may be heard in "Do-Re-Mi" from Rodgers and Hammerstein's score for *The Sound of Music*."

I know you're not reading this book for Music Theory 101, but hear me out on this. Just as the do, re, mi scale is basic and essential to music, I believe there are some do, re, mi concepts that are basic and essential to life. They are principles we can plug into our lives and practice on a daily basis that will help us tune up our lives in this sometimes very out-of-tune world.

DO THE RIGHT THING

Let's begin at the very beginning—just as Maria von Trapp in the movie taught us—with "do." It is spelled *d-o*, and that is the first word of our first principle: *Do the right thing*. There was an interesting book written several years ago by James Patterson and Peter Kim entitled *The Day America Told the Truth* (1995). In that book, average Americans were surveyed on a number of different topics. One of the questions they were asked was "What would you be willing to do for ten million dollars?" The answers were staggering. Seven percent said they would murder someone. Six percent said they would change their race. Four percent said they would change their gender. And 16 percent of those Americans said they would leave their spouse for ten million dollars. Now, you may be thinking, *On certain days, I'd be tempted to do that for a whole lot less!* Thank God, we have the prefrontal cortex in our brains that prevents us from acting on every impulse.

When I first read those statistics, I thought, *Wait a minute . . . this is America. Whatever happened to our character? Whatever happened to our integrity? Whatever happened to just plain doing the right thing?* I think you'll agree with me that sometimes doing the right thing means we have to dig way down deep inside ourselves and tap that "moral compass," as the late author Steven Covey called it. Sometimes it takes every ounce of courage, integrity, and character we can muster to make the right choice and do the right thing. It can be very tempting to make the easy choice instead of the right choice, especially when the easy choice comes packed with millions of dollars.

I found myself in a situation very much like that back in the mid-1970s. This was not a hypothetical survey question for a book; it was my real-life question, and it went exactly like this: "LaDonna, what would you be willing to do for a career in country music?" You see, I had just recorded a record with my brothers on a major label in Nashville. The single off that record went on to win a Grammy Award the following year. But right in the middle of making all that music with my brothers, something happened that completely changed my perspective on life, not to mention my career. I got married! Even though I loved making music with my brothers, I loved making out with my husband a whole lot more. Being on the road 250 days a year on one of those customized tour buses just wouldn't work. Chasing a country music career around with my brothers was not going to be conducive to the kind of marriage I wanted to build with my new husband, Tim Johnson.

As I would experience many times later in life, and as I'm certain you've experienced in your life, I was at a crossroads. I had to dig very deep to make the right choice and do the right thing. Finally, after thought, prayer, and wise counsel from time-tested family and friends, we made the decision to leave the group. It was tough, to say the least. The bullet points for the next few years of my life would go something like this:

- My brothers went on to produce hit records.

- I went on to produce two kids.

- My brothers got famous.

- I got stretch marks!

Simply put, I made what was the right decision for me because I had a *different* song to sing, a *different* path to follow. Unfortunately, my big brother Larry and I didn't talk about my leaving the group until some fifteen years later. It was a spring afternoon in 1991. Tim and I were living in the beautiful Piney Woods section of East Texas at the time. My telephone rang, and it was big brother Larry on the other end of the phone. He said, "LaDonna, I've been walking around out here on my farm in Nashville and I've been talking to God. Guess what God said?"

To say this got my attention would be an understatement. As I shared earlier in the book, Larry has always been one of my heroes. The strain caused by my "defection" from the Gatlin family group has always made me sad. With hopeful anticipation I said, "Larry, I'm all ears!"

He replied, "Well, God said, 'Stupid, go call your little sister!'"

I thought, *Wow! That* must *have been God!*

Larry went on to say, "Sis, when you left the group all those years ago, I thought you had lost your mind. I didn't understand how anybody in her right mind could give up all that country music had to offer us at the time. But here we are fifteen years down the road, and I've been through a few things in my life." He was referring to his own recovery process from drug addiction and alcoholism. Let me note here that Larry has been clean and sober for more than thirty years! You go, Larry!

He went on to say, "Sis, I just needed to call you today and say not only do I understand why you made that decision so many years ago, but *you did the right thing.*"

Hearing those five words meant the world to me. The fact that they came fifteen years later made it even sweeter. But the story doesn't end there. Here's the point—one decision can change the course of your life *forever!*

In 1945 a woman and her son walked into a hardware store in Tupelo, Mississippi, to buy a bicycle for his tenth birthday. However, as they entered the store, the young boy fixated on a

.22-caliber rifle instead. A store clerk showed him the rifle first, but seeing his mother's angst, pulled a guitar out of the display case for the young man to look at. The clerk let him play with the guitar for some time. The boy's interest was more than captured by the instrument, but he didn't have enough money to buy it, which was only $7.75 plus 2 percent sales tax. He'd earned a small amount of money running errands and doing chores, but not nearly enough for the now-prized guitar. Sensing an opportunity to make the best of a tense situation, his mother made a decision. She told him if he would buy the guitar instead of the rifle, she would pay the difference. She did. That young man's name was Elvis Presley.

On December 1, 1955, a woman stepped onto a city bus in Montgomery, Alabama. She was weary from a long day of work and even wearier of the unjust segregation laws in America at that time. On that day Rosa Parks made a decision. She chose *not* to give up her bus seat to a white passenger . . . and the rest is history. She's been called the mother of the civil rights movement and has been named one of the Most Influential Persons of the Twentieth Century—all because she made a decision. Rosa Parks rode that bus in 1955. Lyndon Johnson didn't sign the Civil Rights Act into law until 1964. Oh, the power of one decision!

Here's another example of a mom who didn't have it easy, as recounted by babble.com blogger Jen Chaney and *New York Times* writer Michael Winetrip. Following a divorce, this mom raised three kids as a single parent. When her son (who was a budding athlete) was in fifth grade, she learned he might have attention deficit hyperactivity disorder (ADHD). Several important decisions lay before her, decisions that would forever impact her son.

First, she chose to ignore the all the naysayers. As an educator herself, she listened intently and took it to heart when teachers told her that her son was having problems in school. But she didn't accept one teacher's assessment that "Your son will never be able to focus on anything." She heard those words but didn't accept the message. Instead, she focused her energies and efforts on figuring out how to help her son.

Medical professionals advised stimulant medication for her son; while it did improve his ability to focus, there was not as much of a change as they had hoped for. After two years on medication, her son wanted to stop taking it because he always had to go to the nurse at lunchtime for his pill, which made him uncomfortable. She "heard" her son and gave him the wonderful gift of being listened to. For kids, just knowing that they have a "voice" and that their feelings are valid and considered is a huge setup for success later in life. His mom listened. After consulting with the doctor, she took him off the meds. While kids don't always know what's best for them, allowing him to play a role in making decisions about his life created a deep level of trust between him and his mom.

Determined to help in any way she could, she played to his strengths. When he had trouble focusing on reading, she gave him the sports pages. As he focused on swimming and excelled in the sport, she encouraged him. The result? The distractible little boy for whom many predicted failure became one of the all-time great (if not the greatest) swimmers in history. His name is Michael Phelps.

Michael's mom, Deborah, has every reason to be enormously proud of her son. But I hope she is also very proud of herself. Even though she must have faced plenty of self-doubt, she made some tough decisions that changed her son's life forever.

Whether it's the "biggies" or the seemingly small, almost insignificant ones we make every day, it's the decisions we make that impact our lives and the lives of those we love. Think about it: How many decisions do you make in a day? Every single one has some effect. It's like the bumper car rides at the amusement park; each decision bumps into another and the chain reaction changes everyone's path. Whose path did you change today—and who changed yours? Your life can change, forever, with one decision to *do the right thing*!

In the Christian faith there is much talk about the eternal impact of decisions. What we believe is often the driving force behind our most critical decisions; I know it has been for Tim and me. Some "belief-driven" decisions have incredible power—and it's not always a positive power. Consider the terrorists who sacrifice their very lives in what they consider to be a "holy war." They believe their eternal rewards outweigh the value of their lives or any moral obligation to respect the lives of others. What they believe is the compelling force behind what they do.

Terrorism is an extreme, albeit deadly, example, but there are decisions we make every day that shape our destinies in powerful ways. Every day we decide what to eat. High-calorie, fat-laden foods produce one result, while healthier choices produce another. We decide how to invest our money. Some save, some spend recklessly, and others rarely give it much thought. The decisions we make all have consequences. It's important to clarify what you believe as you make decisions, big and small. Your beliefs, the things you hold as true, influence your actions. Very often, our beliefs are shaken, or at least called into question, as reality forces us to key decision points.

Consider the story of my coauthor, Dr. Mike Marino. In his midtwenties Mike had achieved much of what he thought would bring him happiness, purpose, and success in life. He was using his musical talents to make a fine living and experience what most would consider an exciting and fulfilling life. He was a member of a famous musical group (remember the McCoys's "Hang on Sloopy"?), he was performing all over the world, and he had access to all the "benefits" show business offers a young man. He lived in exciting Las Vegas; he had his pick of women (especially those beautiful Vegas showgirls) and had very little responsibility, except for showing up on time and performing well.

Still, he found his life sad and unfulfilling. His pursuit of stardom had left him directionless, without meaning, purpose, or passion in his life. No amount of applause, recognition, women, or money seemed to satisfy. On a cold December evening, in a hotel room in South Dakota, he reached a decision point. After an evening performance, he turned on the TV to find a man explaining the gospel of Christ. Having been a marginally practicing Catholic in his youth, he never made much time for religious thought. He'd gone through the motions at church without ever questioning what he truly believed.

As he listened to the simple explanation of what it meant to be a Christian, he became intrigued. He prayed with the man on the TV to invite Christ into his life and accept the grace and forgiveness of God. An interesting thing happened. As he prayed he began to weep, almost uncontrollably. He thought, *Why am I crying like this? I don't know why.*

When the prayer concluded, the man on TV said, "Now, some of you are crying and you don't know why. That's the Holy Spirit of God working in your life."

Mike thought, *Wow, there must be something to this!* He would be the first to tell you that no great lightning flashed from heaven, and his life did not immediately turn from sad to happy. But the decision he made that day had an impact that has rippled out to the lives of millions over the thirty-plus years since that day. His journey has been remarkable. He is one of those rare men of faith who operates comfortably in both the faith and secular communities. He has shared his story with millions on radio and in print. He has worked with such luminaries as Dr. Billy Graham, Dr. Laura Schlessinger, medical-pioneering psychiatrist Dr. Daniel Amen, and countless others in his live speaking events. He also counsels corporations and government agencies concerning employee mental health.

The legacy of his simple decision continues to this day. He'd say he's most proud of what he considers his greatest accomplishment—raising three wonderful kids as a single parent and seeing them succeed in this volatile and sometimes challenging world. And this is all because of his decision on that wintry night that helped him find a purpose and destination for his life. Never in his wildest imagination did he dream of the impact that one decision would have.

That's the thing about the decisions we make—we don't really know the outcome until they play out, and sometimes it takes years. Sometimes you just make the best decision you can and live with the outcome. Hall of Fame baseball legend Yogi Berra may have said it best with one of his famous "Yogi-isms": "When you come to a fork in the road, take it!" At first glance, like many of Yogi's comments, that seems a bit nonsensical. What I think he was saying is that we all reach decision moments in life, moments when we must choose one way or another. Given thought, information, prayer, and wise counsel, I've found it's better to make a decision than remain in limbo. I'm not suggesting rushing things, but at some point making a decision gets you unstuck. I've known people who remained in unhappy, unfruitful, and even harmful situations for years, simply because they lacked the internal structure to make a decision that could potentially change things.

As with everything else in life, when we lack the internal structure to make decisions, it's helpful to look for some external structure. When Tim and I made the hard decision to leave the Gatlin family group, we did not do it in a vacuum. We pulled in every bit of sound thinking, advice, and prayer support we could. Flying solo at decision time can be risky business. Let's break it down to a few necessary components for making a decision.

- **Clarify what you believe.** Do you believe in right and wrong? If so, where do you draw the line? How did you arrive at your beliefs? Many times we just "inherit" our beliefs and adopt things we've been taught or had modeled as our own. Perhaps you've been taught very good and productive means for arriving at decisions. Perhaps not. Our view of the world is influenced by what we've been told and what we've experienced. Clarifying what you truly believe and why you believe it will help you as you make life's inevitable decisions.

- **Get information.** A decision made with incomplete or inaccurate information is rarely the best decision. Informed decision making is the path to doing the right thing. How can you truly weigh your options if you haven't considered what they are? Wisdom and good decisions made with good information have been prized possessions since the beginning of time. Scriptures speak hundreds of times about the high value of wisdom. Proverbs 2:2 says, "[Make] your ear attentive to wisdom and [incline] your heart to understanding" (ESV). This thought is mirrored in Ecclesiastes 4:13, which says, "A poor yet wise lad is better than an old and foolish king who no longer knows how to receive instruction" (NASB). Solid information will help you make good decisions.

- **Seek wise counsel.** As I shared, Tim and I did not make our life-altering decision to walk away from country music stardom by ourselves. We sought advice from those who had gone before us. Of course, you have to be careful about whom you seek advice from. Opinions are like noses—everybody has one. Still, it's important to bolster your decision making with safe, sane people who have your best interest at heart. If the trusted voices in your life are seeing a "red flag," you'll want to consider what they're saying. Again, Scripture addresses the concept of a community of support repeatedly. Proverbs 15:22 says, "Without consultation, plans are frustrated, but with many counselors they succeed" (NASB).

Don't fall into the trap of rejecting good advice.
At least consider it; at the end of the day the
decision is still yours.

- **Pray.** Now, if you don't believe God exists, this
  is not going to provide much help. Or perhaps
  you believe in some kind of God but are not sure
  if he/she/it is concerned with your situation.
  Very often our perception of God is based on
  some earthly reflection of authority, like a parent,
  pastor, priest, rabbi, or other role model. Again,
  it's important to clarify what you believe, because
  if you believe that God exists, that Scripture is
  true, and that he loves you, you'll want to seek his
  help and wisdom. The New Testament book of
  James 1:5 says, "But if any of you lacks wisdom,
  let him ask of God, who gives to all generously
  and without reproach, and it will be given to him"
  (NASB). Do you believe that scripture is true?
  If so, make prayer a part of your decision making.
  Tim and I have found that God answers prayer.

One great example of someone who applied these principles concerning a big decision was Pamela. She and her husband, Robert, were Christian missionaries living in the Philippines. While Pamela was pregnant with what would be their fifth child, she suffered a life-threatening infection caused by a pathogenic amoeba. Because of the drugs used to awaken her from a coma and to treat her dysentery, her child in the womb experienced a severe placental abruption. Doctors expected a stillbirth and recommended an abortion to protect Pam's life. Certainly people would have understood—Pamela's life was in danger and the doctors expected the baby to be stillborn anyway. But Pamela was clear about what she believed. She believed the sanctity of the womb was God's solemn direction. She was willing to risk her life if there was a chance her baby within could survive. She and her husband gathered all the information they could from the doctors. At the end of the day they determined that the doctors simply did not know if she or the baby would survive, but they did say there was a chance.

Being missionaries, Pamela and Robert had a strong community of people who loved them enough to tell them the truth. As they laid out the situation for their friends, they found agreement with the decision to honor their commitment to life. Finally, as they and their supporters prayed and sought God's direction for the decision, a peace settled in their hearts and minds. They decided to trust God with the outcome. Pamela gave birth to a healthy baby boy. Oh yes, a few other things followed. That boy grew up to be arguably the greatest college football player in history: Heisman Trophy winner, collegiate national champion, and now NFL quarterback Tim Tebow. Tim has been a positive role model for millions of young men and women. It all started with Pamela and Robert's decision. Who could have imagined the outcome at the time? It's likely that your everyday decisions have consequences far beyond what you can see right now.

Most of the time doing the right thing and making the hard decision is a process, as described earlier. But what if you don't have the luxury of time? Occasionally circumstances force us to make snap decisions and judgments that may have long-lasting implications. It would be great if we could always carefully, thoughtfully, and prayerfully consider the choices when we act, but it just doesn't always work out that way.

In a perfect world we'd all prefer the option to *respond* to life's challenges instead of being forced to *react* to them. A response can be planned, tested, and implemented with forethought. Our reactions, however, reveal more of who we are, or at least what's going on in our bodies, minds, and spirits at the critical decision moment. When we're forced to react in the moment, a light is shined on our core values.

Think about it like a battle. It's easy to be brave during basic training, but a soldier's true character is revealed when the real bullets start to fly. How do you react when the pressure is on? Interestingly, some people actually thrive on operating in crisis mode and feel empowered to make better decisions when they have no choice to delay them. People who have a tendency to procrastinate (avoid making decisions at all) will often create a crisis to force themselves into action. Of course, living with someone like that can be taxing, to say the least. Moving from one crisis to another wears everyone out.

If life's inevitable quick decisions have caused you pain and problems, you can actually improve your ability to react well. Think of how quickly a baseball player has to react to hit a 100-mile-per-hour fastball pitch. If you drive a car, you know how quickly things can change on the freeway. Your very life and the lives of those in your car can depend on your instant decisions. How *do* you make good decisions when you don't have the time to prepare? You practice when the pressure is off. You learn to make good, quick decisions by making good, slow decisions.

Baseball players hit tens of thousands of balls in practice every season. Before every game they're out there taking practice swings when nothing is on the line. Their batting stance, muscle movement, hand-eye coordination, and swing become so perfected they wouldn't know how to do it wrong. What makes a good freeway driver? Well, lots of experience sure helps. The confidence you get from managing familiar situations allows you to drive with steady and purposeful movements. But you don't start on the freeways. Most kids learn to drive behind a simulator or in empty parking lots with their parents. The more you do it when the pressure is off, the better you'll react when the pressure is on.

Making good decisions is much the same. The more practice you have in clarifying your beliefs, gathering information, seeking help, and connecting with God, the better equipped you'll be to make the right call when things move more quickly than you'd like.

Let's close this chapter with a quick life inventory and look at how you make decisions. Here are some things to consider if you really want to do the right thing:

- Do I usually make good decisions, or has my decision-making ability (or lack thereof) caused pain and problems in my life?

- Do I have clarity about what I believe concerning my personal values, my purpose in life, and my spiritual beliefs? What do I believe and why do I believe it?

- Who has had great influence in my life? Why?

- Do I have a support community of people who are safe? Who are those people and why do I trust them?

- What has been the hardest decision in my life and why was it hard?

- Whose decision-making ability have I had influence on? Was it a positive and helpful influence?

- What decision would I most like to take back if I could? Why?

- What are the opportunities I have before me right now to make good decisions and do the right thing?

- If money, time, and opportunity were not objects of consideration, what would I decide to do with the rest of my life?

Chapter 3

RE:
REALIZE
YOUR
POTENTIAL

THE NEXT NOTE ON OUR SCALE IS "RE." In our musical acronym, RE represents the noble pursuit to: *Realize your potential and do everything you can to help others reach their potential.* I've been infinitely blessed to have had people around me who believed in me and sprinkled little "confidence McNuggets" into my heart along my journey. It started very early on with my parents, Billie and Curley Gatlin.

Dad married Mom the day after her eighteenth birthday on Sunday morning, December 22, 1946, in a tiny little West Texas church—in between Sunday school and church. (Does that tell you what kind of wedding they had?) My dad became a blue-collar worker in the oil fields of West Texas and my mother became a homemaker.

They moved all over the place following the oil boom in the Permian Basin, but in the process of making a living, they also made a life. They started their family and did so in a very big way! Mom gave birth to all four of us siblings in a span of only six years! Apparently, the concepts of birth control and safe sex were not on their radar screen.

My mother loved music, and she poured her passion into each of us. According to my mother, we were singing in the delivery room. She says when we were born the doctor held us up by our ankles, swatted our little bottoms, and we sang "All the Gold in California." Okay, we moms tend to exaggerate, but yes, we sang from the very start.

When I was only five years old, the Gatlin Quartet won our first talent show at the Ector County Coliseum in Odessa, Texas. First place was a Shetland pony! Can you believe it? An adorable little pony! Sadly, we were to discover that little pony may well have been the meanest animal on God's earth. On top of that, I'm certain my dad must have been thinking, *Great, this is just what we need—another mouth to feed!* Interestingly enough, second place in that talent contest went to a rock-and-roll group who had a lead singer from Wink, Texas. His name was Roy Orbison—yes, *that* Roy Orbison, who went on to become one of the icons of the rock era. Roy's band won a gift certificate to the best Chinese restaurant in town. We were so bummed about that! A nice dinner out would have been a great adventure, but instead we won the meanest pony on God's earth.

By the time I was ten years old, we'd made four records.

Please tell me you remember what records are—those big, black vinyl shiny things with the little hole in the middle. A few years ago my daughter brought a young man to our house who was absolutely clueless about records. He walked into our home and saw two gold records hanging in our office and said, "Dude, those are like the biggest CDs I've ever seen!" Thankfully, my daughter did not marry him.

The summer I turned ten we traveled and performed all across the country, from California to New York. We ended our adventure by singing at the 1964 World's Fair in New York City. Now, this should tell you something about my mom's character and determination. We were never officially invited to sing at the world's fair, but my little five-foot-two-inch, ninety-five-pound mother found the guy who was in charge, got him by the neck, and said, "My kids can sing anybody off that stage up there—you'd better let them do it!" He did, and we brought the house down! That's the kind of "stuff" that was poured into my heart, mind, and soul from the time I was just a youngster. I can never thank my parents enough for the fact that they believed in our potential!

It's a powerful thing to have someone believe in you like that—and everyone isn't as fortunate as I've been. I know that some of you who read this book will not understand what encouragement and nurture from family even feels like.

Perhaps your self-perception has been shaded by hurtful neg-
ativity and criticism. Because you can never be totally objective about yourself, developing a community of safe, healthy
support is essential in realizing your potential. To truly find
your place in this world, to sing your best song, it's helpful to
be in relationship with people who know you well, have your
best interest at heart, and have earned the right to tell you the
truth in love. That may sound like a foreign concept to you.
The supportive family structure I enjoyed is an increasingly
rare commodity these days. Ironically, in this age of fractured
families and instant electronic connection, we're seemingly
less connected from genuine human care. There's good news
though: if you don't have a safe, supportive community, you
can start building one today.

Being part of a community will help you realize your potential and help others do so too. Engaging in community may not
provide the "instant gratification" we've become so accustomed
to, but in the long run you won't regret it. If you are currently
surrounded by support that is more interested in *correction*
than *connection*, it may be time to expand your circle.

Developing helpful, trustworthy relationships takes some
planning and action. One thing for sure, if you do nothing,
nothing will happen. Healthy relationships do not magically
appear from thin air. They are the result of cultivation, much

like a farmer cultivates his crop. At first the farmer toils, preparing the soil and planting the seed. Then the ground is carefully watered and kept free of disease and predators. For a long time the farmer sees very little fruit from his labor. He rests in the assurance that he's taken the necessary steps to produce a vibrant crop and will eventually reap the harvest.

Building healthy relationships is much the same. You have to invest your efforts in "good soil" and plant healthy seeds. Of course, that can seem like an overwhelming task and just another project on your giant pile of undone things. Where the *internal* structure to "plant the crop" doesn't exist, it's always helpful to find an already existing *external* structure to plug into. Many churches or community organizations have connection and support groups that meet regularly. You can often find them on the Internet by typing in "support groups" or "community groups" in (fill in your city) on an Internet search engine.

A word of caution: You'll need to be careful about what you find on the Internet. There are a lot of kooks out there. Support and connection groups run by established organizations, such as hospitals, respected churches, and community help organizations, are usually pretty safe. Your goal is to get to know others and be known at a more intimate and supportive level, which is an important step on your journey to find your purpose and reach your potential.

It's critical to avoid the temptation of adopting a "lone-wolf" mentality. Sometimes that feels like the safe and familiar thing, but the reality is we all need support, encouragement, and wise counsel. As you begin, you may wish to attend functions in larger group settings so you can blend into the crowd. While this may be a good first step, it is not the goal of getting involved in a support fellowship. Dr. Marino says, "The only thing lonelier than being alone is being alone in a crowd. Every loving connection you witness is a cruel reminder of that which you do not possess." At some point you have to take a risk and open up a little.

It's important that you seek to develop a "community" of support because no single person could or should be the sole repository for your thoughts, feelings, and emotions. You will overwhelm them. They'll burn out and eventually disappoint you because they don't have the capacity to be your only safe friend. By the way, that includes spouses.

Another caution: go slowly. Healthy relationships are not built quickly. Trust is built over time. Many people know all the right talk but have trouble when it comes to walking the right walk. When you're shopping for a healthy community of support, you don't want just to listen to what people say. You also want to watch what they do. Actions truly do speak louder than words.

As you're seeking to build a strong, healthy community of support, the healthier you become the more attractive you'll be to healthy, supportive people! Just as hurting people can tend to huddle in a "circle of misery" to compare and reinforce their pain, healthy people tend to gravitate toward one another as well, seeking to build and grow on one another's strengths and to support one another through struggles.

You've probably heard the saying "Rome wasn't built in a day!" Let me rephrase that to say, "Your support community won't be built in a day!" But every day you invest in developing healthy relationships builds on the next. If you can begin to make a friend this month, they may have other friends that have already stood the test of time. You may find an even safer, saner connection in their circle of support.

Let's break it down to some concrete action steps. Before you start on your journey to develop a safe, sane community of support, it's important to establish a picture of what that would look like. Make a list of some of the essential characteristics of the type of group you'd like to connect with. For example, you may wish to find:

- People who are interested in personal growth. Not just those who are there to complain or "fix" others. Now, every group has some people like this; you just don't want that to be the overriding tone of the time you're investing.

- People in a similar age-group as yours or who have some common life experiences. While the quest for potential and significance crosses all age, racial, and economic barriers, you may "connect" better if at least some of the group fit into your general age and life experience range.

- People who live fairly close, so you won't have the barrier of distance to give you an excuse for not getting together when you don't feel like it.

- A group that offers information that is presented in a manner that you personally find helpful. For instance, if Spanish is your first language, you may find a Spanish-speaking group or leader to be the best fit for you.

- A group that has some emphasis on building relationships within the group.

- A group that has some established history, where you can meet people who may be a little farther down the road than you in their journey.

Once you have a picture in mind of what and who you're looking for, you'll find it easier to target your efforts. Rather than taking a "ready, fire, aim" approach, you'll want to aim first and take some time on the front end to find a structure that has the best chance of success for you.

Sometimes you can find helpful support in places you never thought to look. People who could become vital parts of your life may be right under your nose and you aren't even seeing them. For example, maybe you have neighbors whom you could slowly and carefully get to know better. As I shared before, we are increasingly less connected as a society. I've spoken to many people who have lived in a house or apartment for years and still don't know their next-door neighbors.

Perhaps you've been wounded by people you should have been able to trust, and you've developed a greater tendency to pull inward. That's very common and totally understandable. Past hurts tend to have current effects. It may be very difficult for you to put out that friendly, neighborly "vibe" that might open the door to help. A small, calculated risk might be an evening walk in your neighborhood (providing it is safe).

You'll almost assuredly pass people, and if you smile and say hi, you might be surprised at their reaction. It's not as though most people don't want connection. Unfortunately, our busyness and fear often keep us from taking those small risks and reaching out.

What about your coworkers? Do some of them get together outside of work to foster their relationships on a deeper level? Perhaps some subtle inquiry might lead you to a whole new level of relationship with people whom you only know in the work setting. In my experience most people are fairly guarded at work and don't really open up because it's not always safe. They save their "real self" for more tested relationships that involve nonwork settings, like a company bowling team or company-sponsored community work projects. You might be surprised to find that the people you work with all have meaningful lives and stories that are not a part of how you know them now.

Community work projects are another great place to "fish" for healthy relationships. Most established helping organizations are always on the hunt for volunteers to help. Organizations like Habitat for Humanity, the Red Cross, local hospitals, or the Salvation Army would love to invite you to be a part of what they're doing.

As you reach out and begin to give of yourself, you'll find this is a helpful exercise in discovering who you are and what you want to do with your life. Getting out of yourself and into someone else for a while will help shape a more healthy perspective for your thinking patterns. And, again, you'll open the door to meeting people who may ultimately become vital members of your support team.

If you're going to develop a helpful community, you are going to have to take small, measured risks. It's sometimes helpful to take five minutes and write out a plan. For example, *Today I am going to the gym and I'm going to say hi to at least three people. If any of them respond in a friendly manner, I'm going to introduce myself by my first name.* Now, don't set yourself up for failure by making your plan too detailed or predicting the outcome. Just keep it simple with no expectation other than taking a few small risks yourself.

This may feel really scary for you. I understand. But if you stay in your house and watch TV or surf the Internet, you are not going to develop a community of support, and a community of support is essential to realizing your potential. You cannot do this by yourself. Life just doesn't work that way—it never has and never will. You will need the love and encouragement of safe, sane people in your life. Let's consider what they look like:

- **Safe, sane people are interested in their personal growth.** As you begin to mature, you realize that when you're standing still in life, you're really moving backward, because life is moving forward and you have to move to keep up. You'll do better if you surround yourself with people who recognize that they've not yet reached their full potential and still have more of life and learning to embrace.

- **Safe, sane people are genuinely interested in others.** If your relationship is going to develop into one of mutual care and respect, it's important to connect with people who don't always make it about themselves. Healthy relationships involve the ability to see things from more than just your point of view. If you want to attract people like this, be one of them. As the relationship develops, watch for signs that it's too one-sided. The last thing you need is to be a full-time emotional garbage can for someone else.

- **Safe, sane people talk *and* listen.** We all have different personalities. Some are more inclined to talk than others. From a brain science perspective, women generally use far more words than men. They have language on both sides of their brains; men only have it on one. Whether you're a talker or not, you do have to talk to be in a relationship. If the relationship involves one person who does all the talking and the other does all the listening, it will not stand the test of time. Dr. Marino will tell you that one of the common complaints he hears from clients is that no one listens and understands their problems. Rather than finding people to tell you what you need to do, it's often more helpful to connect with people who will just listen and sit with you. *Presence* trumps *presents* when it comes to helpful relationships.

- **Safe, sane people do not embrace gossip.** If the people in your community of support are consistently talking with you about others in the community, rest assured they are talking about you behind your back as well. While safe communities sometimes involve confrontation, it should be done with all the involved people present and in the spirit of building up, not tearing down. Trust breeds confidence and courage. Knowing you have people in your corner equips you to reach for the stars.

- **Safe, sane people tell you what *they* need, not what *you* need.** One of the great skills that comes from involvement in a safe, sane community is learning to articulate what you want. Many have never developed an "adult voice" that feels it's okay to ask for what you need. With all respect to the great magicians of the world, no one can read minds. How will people know how to treat you if you don't tell them? How will you know how to treat others if they don't tell you? Part of safe support involves feeling the freedom to ask for what you want without judgment or punishment. If you feel diminished or shamed when you ask for what you want, you may be asking the wrong people. They may not have the capacity to give you what you need. It's their problem, not yours.

- **Safe, sane people make themselves reasonably available.** No one can be your 24/7 lifeline, but if you're connected to a caring group of people, it is reasonable to expect them to be there for you. And it's just as reasonable for them to expect the same from you. If calls go consistently unreturned or there is a sense that others are avoiding you, it's time to clear the air and ask if there's a problem. If you just sit with the uncertainty, you'll manufacture all sorts of reasons in your head like, "They must not like me," or "I must have offended them." In reality, it may be that they didn't get the message or they had an urgent situation that monopolized their time. More likely than not, it had nothing to do with you. You won't know unless you ask. If it turns out that you really are bugging them too much and that's driving them away, it's time to ask yourself this question: *Do I need that person too much?* If you need any person too much, even a spouse, the relationship will not be healthy and healing for either side. That's why I stress the need for "community," because you need a team to reach your potential.

- **Safe, sane people know other safe, sane people.** One of the great ways to recognize safe, sane people is that they, themselves, are plugged into

other safe, sane people. You may look upon them
with envy as you see them interacting with others
in caring and helpful ways. Instead of looking
on from afar, nudge closer. Don't be afraid to tell
them how much you admire their circle of support. Go slowly—you don't want to push your
way into the circle—but making yourself available
to it and articulating your desire for closer, meaningful relationships may very well open the door.
Sometimes you just have to ask.

Please don't wait; you can do something today to begin to
find a support system that will be invaluable in reaching your
potential. Call a well-known church, hospital, or helping organization and ask what they have to offer. Community support
groups are usually free; all you're investing is your time. Volunteer to feed the poor, plant trees, work at a blood drive, or go on
a church mission trip. Yes, reaching out involves some risk, but
the self-discovery and ultimate payoff is worth it.

One other thing: as you plug into a community, you'll
soon discover that your involvement is a two-way street. They
need you just as much as you need them. You may not believe
it today, but *you* have a lot to offer! Healthy, safe people are
waiting to meet you. Life is short—what are you waiting for?

It's never too late. Consider this story about my parents: Mom and Dad live right across the street from Tim and me. Today, in their eighties, my parents still maintain that same strong belief in us kids. Their encouragement has been, and always will be, a key factor in the Gatlin kids' success. It was their unconditional love that allowed us to take risks without fear. We always knew we had their support, no matter what. Little did Tim and I know that we would have a chance to "pay it forward" to our own family so soon. We live in what is marketed as a "Premier Adult Active Community." That's code for you have to be fifty-five or older to live here! The one phrase in the homeowner's contract that sealed the deal for me was "This is an age-restricted community. Your adult children may never come back and live with you again!"

That phrase is particularly significant to me because Tim and I are grandparents now. To date, we have five precious grandkids—what an incredible blessing. Our first grandchild came to us in a very unexpected way. Our daughter, Annie, had him two months after she graduated from high school. Obviously, this was not in our game plan. We thought we were about to become "empty nesters," but that wasn't to be; so we changed the plan. And, as any Texan can tell you, "changing horses in the middle of a stream" can be quite an experience. That's the interesting thing I've learned about unplanned changes. You can fight them and get bruised and bitter, or you can accept the situation and look for the potential good. As the saying goes, "When you argue with reality, you lose . . . but only 100 percent of the time."

Our first grandchild, Hayden Russell Foster, was born on July 12, 2000—eight and a half pounds of pure joy! We affectionately called him the "Bugerhead," and believe me, he still lives up to his name on a daily basis. He's *all* boy! We brought Annie and Hayden home from the hospital to live with us (this was prior to the "age-restricted community" days) and began an incredible journey.

Annie went to college to become a teacher. Between her studies, my one-hundred-days-a-year-on-the-road speaking schedule, and Tim's job as a worship pastor, it was "all hands on deck" to raise and nurture this precious little boy. We enlarged our residential square footage to accommodate Annie and Hayden; but when you have three generations living under the same roof, I'm not sure even the White House would have enough physical, practical, and emotional "space."

Suffice it to say, it was a challenge, but unexpected good things surfaced. Those years with Annie and Hayden in our home taught me so much about authentically "walking my talk." I discovered the personal benefits of helping people reach their potential. I affirmed in my heart what I suspect my parents had discovered long ago. Investing my life in Annie and Hayden's success was more than worth the changes we had to make. It moved Tim and me beyond our comfort zone again, just like years before when we left the Gatlin family group.

I'll never forget a pivotal moment in that journey. Hayden was three years old at the time, but he wasn't yet potty trained. (Warning: marginally PG-rated potty talk ahead—can we just be frank here?) We had done everything we knew to accomplish this milestone event, but to no avail. Being the "hip" grandmother that I was, I "Googled" the term *potty chair.* It immediately sent me to the Target website where I read all about a state-of-the-art potty chair that played music when the desired feat is accomplished! Ain't technology great? As you can imagine, I rushed to Target, bought the miracle potty chair, brought it home, and set it up in the bathroom. I brought Hayden in and poured some water into the chair. The music blared and it scared him to death! He ran out of the bathroom as quickly as he could. Obviously, the "singing potty chair" was a total bust for Hayden. Desperate, I did what any committed grandma would do in that situation—I bribed him! I gave him an M&M if he would use it! This worked a bit better, but he still wasn't getting the hang of it.

Early one Sunday morning, I was "seated" in my master bathroom. Okay, that's as graphic as I'll get—you fill in the blanks. All of a sudden I realized I'd left the bathroom door wide open totally by accident. *No big deal,* I thought, *Hayden and Annie are asleep upstairs. Tim has already left for an early morning sound check at church. I'll get on with my business, get on with my day, and no one will be the wiser, right?* Wrong! The very moment that thought entered my mind, I heard tiny footsteps coming down the staircase—and there he was. Little Hayden stood before me. As only a three-year-old can, he inquisitively peered into the bathroom. His eyes got huge and he whispered, "Nannie, are you doing your business?" I replied, "Yes, I am!" (What was I going to say, "No, I'm baking cookies"?)

At my reply, Hayden very reverently began to back out of the toilet area as if he were thinking, *This is holy ground and I have disturbed something sacred.* I was somewhat relieved, because I thought at least Hayden knew that when you do your business, you need privacy. This felt like a tiny step in the right direction toward our potty-training goal.

Just as that thought crossed my brain, Hayden reappeared from around the corner and screamed at the top of his lungs, in his most excited voice, "Nannie, I'm so proud of you!" Then he gave me an M&M!

Who learned the lesson that day? Nannie did. I learned three lessons, not just one:

1. LaDonna, use your common sense and shut the bathroom door.

2. Sometimes embarrassing, even humiliating circumstances can teach us invaluable lessons.

3. Out of the mouth of babes comes profound truth. Five words from a three-year-old reminded me of something we never outgrow the need to hear: "I'm so proud of you!"

Hayden taught me about the incredible power of encouragement, of truly believing in someone and letting them know it in no uncertain terms. Who in your world today might need to hear those words from you? Your spouse, your children, perhaps yourself? Only you know the answer to that. All I know is this: it works. Believing in people and letting them know it is a powerful thing! There's no question about it, I would not be where I am today were it not for people who believed in me along the way.

Scripture talks much about the power of encouragement:

- Proverbs 3:27 says, "Never walk away from someone who deserves help; your hand is God's hand for that person" (MSG).

- In 1 Thessalonians 5:11, Paul instructed the early church in this way: "So speak encouraging words to one another. Build up hope so you'll all be together in this, no one left out, no one left behind. I know you're already doing this; just keep on doing it" (MSG).

- Wise King Solomon, one of the early Scripture writers, spoke of this fact nearly three thousand years ago when he talked about the value of a community of support. The man touted as the wisest on earth said, "Two people are better off than one, for they can help each other succeed. If one person falls, the other can reach out and help. But someone who falls alone is in real trouble. Likewise, two people lying close together can keep each other warm. But how can one be warm alone? A person standing alone can be attacked and defeated, but two can stand back-to-back and conquer. Three are even better, for a triple-braided cord is not easily broken!" (Eccl. 4:9–12 NLT).

Truly, the power of encouragement has stood the test of time. Both the Old and New Testaments of the Christian faith are dotted with examples of the value of a supportive community, as are the sacred texts of most major religions. In the very beginning in Genesis God said, "It is not good for man to be alone (Gen. 2:18)."

Whether you count yourself as a believer or a skeptic, it is hard to make a case for a life of solitude as the path to fulfillment, freedom, and purpose. I have never observed or even heard of anyone (apart from genuine sociopaths) who didn't at their core desire deep, meaningful, loving relationships.

What role does encouragement currently play in your life? As you consider how you might move closer to finding your purpose and meaning, and realizing your God-given potential, answer these questions:

- What do I really enjoy doing?

- What am I really good at?

- What does my current community of support (or lack thereof) look like?

- Is it helpful or not?

- Who, if anyone, has been an encourager in my life?

- How could I expand my circle of support in the next weeks and months ahead?

- What would be my very first step in doing so?

- To whom could I reach out with an encouraging word or action today?

Chapter 4

MI:
MIND YOUR
MANNERS

GOOD MANNERS JUST AREN'T what they used to be. Our increasing focus on e-mail, text messages, and various social media outlets seems to have left us virtually oblivious to the actual human beings around us. And as we take our personal lives with us everywhere we go, engaging with others about *their* lives drifts toward the "back burner" of our priority list.

It's easy to forget to say "please" and "thank you" when your cell phone app is telling you to *turn left here!* Staying connected to reality and real people can be a challenge when the "virtual" world is at our fingertips. In a sense, we have settled for a "wax museum" life stance. When we can't have the real experience, we accept a close replica. Think about it—when was the last time you sat down for a leisurely time of good conversation and connection with people you truly care about? For most of us, those "community" moments are too few and far between. The tyranny of the urgent has become so overwhelming that moving from crisis to crisis has almost become the norm.

What happened? In just a generation we've gone from families that sat around the TV set to *Sing Along with Mitch* (younger readers, look it up on the Internet, please!) to families where each person retires to their private area to "connect" with others in cyberspace or watch any one of 900 choices on TV in high definition. The art of human interaction is dying, and that's sad because, as I shared in Chapter 3, we are not designed to be alone.

Just a few years ago most people in America would know what you were talking about if you said, "Remember the Golden Rule!" Young people today might think you were talking about the amount of "bling" you could accumulate in gold chains and earrings, but that's not what I'm talking about. For centuries the Golden Rule has been our reference to the Christian scripture found in Matthew 7:12 that instructs us, "In everything, do to others what you would have them do to you."

I believe the practice of treating others the way you want to be treated is a key first step in reconnecting with a healthy community of real people. It's how we're designed to live and thrive in this difficult world. Interestingly, the Golden Rule exists in one form or another in almost all cultures.

The value of treating others as you'd like to be treated extends far beyond the pale of orthodox Christianity. The texts of most major religions contain similar admonitions. Frankly, what's true is true, wherever it's stated.

- Judaism: "What is hateful to you, do not do to your fellow man. This is the entire Law; all the rest is commentary."

- Buddhism: "Hurt not others with that which pains yourself."

- Hinduism: "This is the sum of duty; do naught unto others what you would not have them do unto you."

- Confucianism: "What you do not want done to yourself, do not do to others."

- Islam: "No one of you is a believer until he loves for his neighbor what he loves for himself."

- Baha'i: "And if thine eyes be turned toward justice, choose thou for thy neighbor that which thou choosest for thyself."

- Jainism: "A man should wander about treating all creatures as he himself would be treated."

- Yoruba Proverb (Nigeria): "One going to take a pointed stick to pinch a baby bird should first try it on himself to feel how it hurts."

This last one is one of my favorites! Wouldn't our world change for the better if we all practiced that?

Even those leading the charge of cutting-edge technology have begun to embrace the downside of limiting actual human interaction. Former Google CEO Eric Schmidt reinforced the importance of tuning in to others recently when he gave the commencement address at University of Pennsylvania. In his remarks, he first admonished the graduating class to use today's technology to its greatest potential and to never be afraid of learning and embracing new advancements. He acknowledged that they were, in fact, taking his advice at that very moment as he could see them texting each other across the aisle as he spoke!

However, he ended his remarks by asking, "What is the real meaning of life? In a world where everything is remembered and everything is kept forever, the world we are in, you need to live for the future . . . the things you really care about. What are those things?"

He continued, "In order to find out . . . you need to turn OFF your computers and cell phones. In doing so we find that, among other things, people are really the same all around the world. We really do care about the same things."

Wow! You're kidding, right? Turn it off? Surely not—but that's exactly what he said. Schmidt concluded, "You will never know a joy greater than holding the hand of your grandchild as he takes his first steps."

I believe he was reminding us that nothing, absolutely nothing can replicate the power of one-on-one connection with another human being. As you seek to find meaning and purpose in your life, the value of engaging with a safe, supportive community of real-life humans cannot be overstated. If you desire to truly glean the good things from life, it is not optional.

Another core life principle that seems lost today is placing a high value on truth. Unfortunately, some of our politicians, business leaders, and even some of our faith leaders have "spun" the truth to suit their agenda. One political party calls something good, while another proclaims the very same thing is bad. Which is true? Or perhaps neither is true and the real truth lies somewhere in the middle. In this day of our twenty-four-hour news cycle and instant information, it's getting pretty hard to find the truth.

In my view, in order to look for and find the truth, we have to actually believe that there are certain things that are true. You've likely heard recent philosophers spout some version of a saying that goes "There are no absolutes." When you think about it, that's a pretty absurd statement, because the statement itself—that there are no absolutes—is an absolute statement. I will grant you that very few things in life happen in the absolute. Most of life happens between one extreme and the other, but clarifying your belief about absolute truth will help you live a better and more engaged life. Do you believe there are some things that are always true?

If you embrace the Christian faith, do you believe that the Bible is absolutely true? If so, that will surely shape the way you conduct your life and relationships. Sometimes I feel sad for people who have nothing dependable, no absolute truths to hold on to in life. Realistically, this life holds a barrelful of trouble for us all. Jesus was very clear about that, when he said, "In this world you will have trouble. But take heart! I have overcome the world (John 16:33)." This reality, that the world is filled with difficulty, is confirmed repeatedly in Christian Scripture. Look at Matthew 6:34, where it says, "Therefore do not worry about tomorrow, for tomorrow will worry about itself. Each day has enough trouble of its own."

However, if you embrace Scripture as truth, there is more to the story. Psalm 27:5 says, "For in the day of trouble he will keep me safe in his dwelling; he will hide me in the shelter of his sacred tent and set me high upon a rock." The psalmist again cries out to God in Psalm 32:7, with this confident plea, "You are my hiding place; you will protect me from trouble and surround me with songs of deliverance."

Now comes the hard question. *What do you believe?* Are there absolute truths in life that are worth living by and defending? Should a parent always care for their child? Is it wrong to break your marriage vows? Will you always crash to the ground when you jump off a high building? Not all moral dilemmas are so clear. What's your plan when the answer is not so obvious? Life is complicated in that much of it involves making decisions that are not quite as easy as challenging the truth of gravity by jumping off a bridge. What's your plan to make productive and God-honoring decisions when the storms hit?

Perhaps starting with a core question will open your thinking. Here's a question you may wish to run your life and decisions through—what is true? What are the nonnegotiables in your life? What do you hold as sacred and always true? Perhaps the honest answer to that question is that you're not sure. Clarifying that thinking will bring clarity to your life. I guarantee it.

You will begin to treat others in a manner that reflects your worldview of what is right and what is wrong. In doing so you'll teach them how to treat you. If you want your kids to embrace healthy, unshakable values that honor life, God, and others, show them how. The first step is getting it settled in your mind by asking, "What is true about my life, my beliefs, my purpose, and my passion?"

Once you've begun to settle your thinking about what you believe, you'll find that supportive actions naturally follow. For example, if you view a homeless drug addict as a person of weak character who is in the street because he's lazy, you'll likely walk by with a nasty look of contempt and refuse to buy into his money-begging pleas.

However, if you view that same homeless person as a creation of God who, through bad decisions or circumstances, now finds himself falling far short of God's plan and purpose for his life, you'll likely take a different action path. The thought, *I'm not going to enable his bad habits* might well be replaced by, *There but for the grace of God go I; did God put this person in my path for a reason?*

Bringing clarity to what you believe to be true (if anything) will affect all of your relationships—from the casual to the most intimate. If you come to the conclusion that our core premise of this chapter is true—that you should treat others as you'd like them to treat you—then every interaction you have is colored by that philosophical paintbrush.

Putting yourself in someone else's shoes and assessing how your words and actions impact others has a remarkable effect. Dr. Marino will tell you that among the most common complaints he hears in his counseling office is that people do not feel heard, seen, or valued in their interactions with family and friends. How would you like to be treated? Would you like to feel heard, seen, and valued? Of course you would—it's the way we're wired.

If that's what you want in your life, model it in your actions with others. Now, not everyone is safe, and they may not respond well to your kindness. Unfortunately, people's life troubles spill out at times; you can't control that. But the best shot you have at moving toward fulfillment and peace with yourself is to treat others based on what you believe to be true. If you think people have value, treat them that way. If you think marriage is sacred, don't violate your vows. If you believe parents should be involved in their kids' education, show up at the PTA meetings. When your actions are consistent with your stated beliefs (stated either publicly or privately), you will live with more confidence and conviction.

Walt Disney stated this concept so well when he said, "When your values are clear, decisions are easy." How clear are your values? When seeking to establish what you hold as true, what you believe, it's a good idea to also look at *why* you believe what you believe. What do you believe and why do you believe it? Upon examination, we often find that many of our core beliefs were just "adopted" from our families or influential others in our lives, like teachers, clergy, coaches, and so on. While that isn't necessarily a bad thing, living your life based on someone else's belief system rarely allows your "self" to develop to maturity.

As a mature adult, it's important to speak with your own voice and act based on what you believe is right—not what is expected of you or what you feel might not disappoint someone else. If you live your life in response to someone else's expectations, you will eventually develop what psychologists call a "hostile resentment" toward that person or persons who control your life. You will not find room for your own thoughts, dreams, and desires.

From a Christian scriptural viewpoint, this is not God's plan. In 1 Corinthians 14:20 the apostle Paul wrote, "Brothers and sisters, stop thinking like children. In regard to evil be infants, but in your thinking be adults." As you begin to treat others in a mature fashion, most will respond by treating you with the same type of respect and honor. As you hear, see, and value others, they are more likely to respond in kind.

Thinking mature, truth-based thoughts and speaking with a mature voice is not easy. For most it is a new experience, and perhaps you've not had many good role models to show you the way. Here are some tips when it comes to thinking and communicating as a mature adult.

A Mature Voice Thinks Before It Speaks

Many times our natural response is to blurt out the first thing that comes to mind as we react to life's bumpy events and people. The part of your brain that governs your impulse control is called the prefrontal cortex. It is in the front part of our brains and extends into the temple areas. It is the human and thoughtful part of our brains, and it keeps us from acting on our every impulse. Chimpanzees are the closest living being to us when it comes to the prefrontal cortex—they have about 16 percent of what we humans have. Dogs have only 7 percent and cats about 3 percent. If you have a cat, you know that they are not known for their impulse control. They are distracted by the slightest movement or sound. If you want them to stop what they're doing, just break out a laser pointer light. They will chase it endlessly up and down the wall (until something else distracts them!).

As previously stated, from a brain science perspective, women use far more words than men. They have language on both sides of their brains, while men have it on only one side. Taking personality and genetics into consideration, some people are just more inclined to talk than others. Wherever you find yourself on the spectrum of talkativeness, it's still important to think before you speak. When you *respond* instead of *react* to others, you'll find you have a better outcome in your relationships. Reaction rarely has a good outcome; thoughtful response is better.

A Mature Voice Uses an
Economy of Words

The more words you use, the less people view you as credible. Overexplaining not only casts doubt on what you're saying, it places you in a "one-down" position where you are seemingly justifying your decision, or even your very existence. The gospel of Matthew addresses this concept when it says, "All you need to say is simply 'Yes' or 'No'; anything beyond this comes from the evil one" (5:37). While it may be appropriate to justify your thinking and behavior to God and those with whom you have intimate relationships, you are not obligated to share your reasoning with the world. Continually trying to do so will leave you with a childlike self-perception, and that's how many others will view and treat you as well.

A Mature Voice Is Trustworthy

As you begin to say what you mean and mean what you say, you'll discover that you *and* others will take you seriously. Do you have a difficult time asking for what you want? That's not uncommon. As your actions consistently match your words, you'll find that people begin to take you seriously and consider how what they do impacts you. As you begin to set clear boundaries regarding what you will and will not accept, people begin to "hear" you. Of course, you don't want to do so in a mean-spirited manner—boundaries are not a hammer. Being clear about what you believe, what your values are, and who you are as a person sets the stage for the mature, adult "you" to emerge.

OUR WORDS HAVE GREAT POWER

The old saying "Sticks and stones may break my bones, but names will never hurt me" is a complete falsehood. Our words have enormous life-giving or life-crushing capabilities. Many who struggle to maintain their adult lives, relationships, and sense of purpose in life are reaping the effects of critical words. When someone who has a position of influence or authority in your life has been exceedingly critical, it is very difficult to develop an adult self that feels free to like what they like and not like what they don't. Critical, shaming words cut to our very core.

Shame is about the defectiveness you feel as a human, as opposed to guilt, which is about something you have done wrong or thought of doing. Shame is not *you've done something bad*; it is *you ARE bad*. People who have experienced shame often feel they are not worthy of love or good things. They live their lives waiting for the next bad thing to happen, like that is what they deserve and should expect.

Most of us have experienced shame in our lives to one degree or another. For many it is the shaming parent or other family member, like a sibling. For others it could have been a teacher, pastor, or other respected person, like a boss or coach—anyone who is in some way related to our self-esteem.

Shame is typically put on us by someone else, but in the long run we begin to put it on ourselves. It's a learned behavior and thinking pattern that becomes familiar and comfortable. You convince yourself that the person who put the shame on you must be right, and you begin to believe and embrace it yourself. People typically respond to shame in different ways:

- **Perfectionism**. Any mistake advertises your imperfection to the world, or so you think. There is a sense that everyone is watching, waiting for you to screw up. The myth is "If I could just be good enough, X would happen." Unfortunately, the measure of what is "good enough" is unclear, and there's a nagging sense that you won't be able to sustain "good enough."

- **Isolation and withdrawal**. Rather than facing the criticism of others, you pull back from doing

anything, believing that you will not succeed
and that you'll be painfully humiliated for
even trying.

- **Exhibitionism**. You flaunt your bad parts to
  create the rejection you have come to expect.
  People with shame-based thinking can tend to
  self-destruct rather than let someone else hurt
  them. Have you ever met someone who couldn't
  wait to *get all their cards on the table?* The sense
  is that they're testing the water to see if their bad
  parts will drive away relationships.

One place to start the healing is to identify the core or root
of the shame. Whom are you getting (or did you get) the shame
from? Whom are you carrying it for? Understanding the root
is essential—most of the time we carry shame for things that
were not our fault or that we had no control over. Unfortunately, as a child, you live in a very black-and-white world and
have a hard time seeing your parents or other authority figures
as bad. Kids are naturally egocentric and see the world through
"me"-colored glasses. That's why kids will defend parents who
are guilty of horrendous behavior and often want to return to
an abusive situation so "they" can make amends. If shame has

been a part of your life, you always feel as though there's something wrong with you.

Correcting that inaccurate thinking is an important step in getting out from underneath the oppression of shame. Once you've identified where the shame has come from, it's time for a reality check. Is the shame you feel really based on your defectiveness? How many times do you think you have to tell someone things like, "You'll never get that right," "You're stupid," "You're ugly," "You're lazy," "You're fat," "You can't do it," *before they believe it?*

Not too many, especially if you hold a position of authority over them. These thought patterns get so ingrained in our heads that they become our automatic thought whenever our worth is challenged. Once you begin to believe these negative things about yourself, you begin to train others to treat you that way. You create the reality you have been led to believe is true.

There's a sense that you don't deserve good things, you are afraid of joy, you are waiting for the bottom to fall out, and you believe that you're not worthy of success. It's as though deep "thought grooves" have been worn into your head and everything falls into the "I am bad" channel. To develop the ability to respect yourself and others, you have to go through a process of unlearning those thought patterns you've been drilled with.

It's like the alphabet. It gets so drilled into your head that you have a difficult time doing it wrong—try it.

This inaccurate thinking often breeds relationship trouble. Shame-filled people do not generally have healthy relationships. They *overreact* to what everyone else is doing and *underreact* to what's going on inside them. They don't feel worthy of self-care and feel that their needs always take second place to others' needs. That's called codependency.

To further complicate matters, people who grow up in shame-filled homes often try to recreate their relationship dynamics with their choice of spouse. Somehow the feeling is that you can get it right this time, and you gravitate to the familiar. *Better the devil you know than the devil you don't* is the saying. It's your comfort zone; it's what you know and what was modeled for you. If you had a critical and abusive parent, you're likely to marry a critical, abusive spouse. Some key points to remember:

- **Shame results in a loss of dignity.** Everyone is born with a sense of *personhood*, which, if properly nurtured, will instinctively help him or her make the right life choices. Some, however, were needlessly shamed in early life and grew up with a sense of loss about their personhood.

- **Shame produces emotional pain.** When a person is shamed, his or her emotions are damaged. This causes a sense of loss, hurt, and devaluation. Sometimes you don't acknowledge the reality of your emotional pain, but ask any physician about the effects of emotional pain. Emotional pain causes a myriad of physical symptoms.

- **Shamed people often medicate their pain.** We humans lick our emotional wounds by medicating our pain through a multitude of means: sports, food, money, sex, television, personal achievements, immoral relationships, drugs, alcohol, tobacco, rage, and various other things. These are all vain attempts to quiet the discomfort.

People who struggle with shame often revert to a "childlike" stance, where they have very poor boundaries with others and rarely speak with an adult voice. An adult uses "I" statements: "I" am willing to do this; "I" am not willing to do that. If shame influences your thinking, your "I" rarely gets a voice.

Developing your "I" voice that speaks as an adult is a process that takes some time. As you begin to retrain your thinking, you will take an occasional step back. That's normal—expect it. The tendency then is to fall into the familiar pattern that suggests that *this will not work for me—nothing ever does.* That, again, is simply an inaccurate thought. If you want to learn to speak as an adult, treat others as you'd want them to treat you, and literally show others how it's done, here are some steps to unplugging shame's influence in your life:

Step 1. Become aware that shame is part of your life and change is possible. Start where you are.

Step 2. Connect to healthy support. Support is essential, especially at the beginning of your journey to emotional and spiritual maturity.

Step 3. Stop minimizing the hurt that's been done to you. Assign appropriate responsibility. I'm not talking about blame; I'm talking about embracing reality. You can't move forward unless you forgive, and you can't forgive unless you first acknowledge the legitimate offense. Get out of the denial trap.

Step 4. Learn how to forgive. Forgiveness is a process involving embracing reality, grieving the genuine losses, understanding how you got to where you are, and ultimately releasing justice to God. Forgiveness does not mean absolving those who've hurt you of responsibility, or even having a relationship with people who've shamed you. Trust has to be earned. Forgiveness is about the past—trust is about the future.

Step 5. Begin to retrain your thinking patterns. When your thoughts fall into the familiar patterns of thinking that say things are not going to work out for you, no one really cares, you are "less than," you are not worthy of love and care—even from yourself—begin to recognize them and challenge them. Ask yourself these questions:

- Is that true?

- How do I know that's true? Can I be sure?

- Whose thought is that really? Whose voice am I hearing? Who says so?

- Apart from my thoughts and what I'm feeling (which are unreliable), what really *is* true?

Your actions, that is to say, your ability to treat others with civility, respect, and dignity, basically stems from your thoughts and feelings. It's important to recognize that how you think and feel pretty much drive what you do. The formula mental health professionals often use is *Thoughts + Feelings = Actions*. If you look at that as a mathematical equation, you'll surmise that changing any one of the integers changes the outcome. If your thoughts change, your feelings and actions will be affected.

Let's look at those components individually. How much control do you have over your *feelings*? None. They are what they are. It's not helpful to hear "Don't feel that way," or "You shouldn't feel that way." Your feelings simply are what they are. What you *can* do with your feelings is to accurately identify them and seek their roots. For example, sometimes we feel angry, but underneath the anger are deep feelings of sadness, hurt, or frustration. Unmasking the true feeling will help you get to its root. Where is that feeling coming from? When have you felt like that in the past? What's driving the feeling?

However, as we addressed earlier in this chapter, you do have some level of control over your *thoughts*. You can challenge them or at least recognize them for what they are. Considering your true thoughts and giving them a place to exist in your personhood can be a very healing experience. Don't fall into the trap of automatically dismissing them or "shoulding" yourself, like, *I shouldn't think that.*

Your *actions*, however, are the things over which you have the most control. When you change your actions, you will begin to change the way you think and feel. Taking small, measured steps to interact with others in helpful and healing ways will open the door for hope and healing in your life as well. You have far more control over your actions than you may think.

Of course, you'll never get it settled in your mind how you should treat others unless you first determine how you want to be treated yourself. It's not selfish, as some in the Christian faith community might suggest, to consider your own desires and needs. If Scripture is true, you are of great value and worthy of care and respect. In fact, the Bible tells us repeatedly to *love our neighbor as we love ourselves*. That exact instruction is found:

- Once in the book of Leviticus

- Three times in the Gospel of Matthew

- Twice in the Gospel of Mark

- Once in the Gospel of Luke

- Once in the book of Romans

- Once in the book of Galatians

- Once in the book of James

How well can you *love your neighbor as you love yourself* if you don't consider yourself worthy of dignity, kindness, and respect? Your words and actions toward others reflect how you perceive yourself and set the tone for how you want to be treated.

As you ponder your manners and the value of the Golden Rule, consider the words of the late Dr. Martin Luther King Jr. Recently, I was retrieving my luggage in the Birmingham, Alabama, airport and I was struck by his words that are engraved on a small granite slab in the baggage area. From a Birmingham jail in 1963, he wrote, "We are caught in an inescapable network of mutuality tied in a single garment of destiny. What affects one directly, affects all indirectly."

As Dr. King so eloquently stated, every human interaction shapes countless lives beyond what we can even imagine. All we truly have of value in this life is our relationship with God and other people. If you'd like to live a more connected, interactive, and fulfilling life, consider these questions:

- How do I treat people?
- Do I believe there are absolute truths? What are they?
- What and *who* are the nonnegotiables in my life?
- Do I feel seen, heard, and loved by others?
- How much has modern technology disconnected me from others?
- Whom would I like to treat better in the future?

- Whom might I need to set healthy boundaries with?

- How much is worry a part of my life? What do I worry about? Does it help?

- Do I speak with a "mature" voice or sometimes revert to a childlike stance? Why?

- Has shame influenced my life? From whom?

- Whom can I encourage today?

Chapter 5

FA:
FAILURES
CAN BECOME
FERTILIZER

L IFE IS, AT BEST, A MIX OF success and failure. The most successful people who've ever lived are usually quick to share that their road to success has been dotted with many failures. Of course, people like Thomas Edison, Henry Ford, Walt Disney, Donald Trump, and Bill Gates seem to have mastered the capacity to view failure as productive experiments in learning. Most of us are not quite as thick-skinned when it comes to failure. Nevertheless, we all experience failure from time to time. Given that reality, how *can* we turn our biggest failures into something that actually enriches our lives and the lives of those around us?

I watched my big brother Larry Gatlin do just that. The decade of the 1980s was huge for our family. The Gatlin Brothers had ten top ten records and two number one hits. They had won pretty much every award there was to win in music—Gold, Platinum, Grammy, Best Country Song category—you name it. The den at Larry's eighty-two-acre spread on the outskirts of Nashville looked like a "famous" museum. Everywhere you looked there was another picture of Larry with somebody really famous. Larry and Elvis, Larry and the president, Larry and Dolly Parton, Larry and the pope—you get the idea. Larry Gatlin had arrived!

Incredibly, it was at this very pinnacle of his career that he found himself crawling around on his hands and knees in a hotel room in Dallas looking for something else to snort up his nose. My brother had become hopelessly addicted to drugs and alcohol. As painful as that moment was—groveling through the carpet, snorting pieces of lint in hopes they were cocaine he'd spilled—it was probably the moment that saved Larry's life.

When Larry tells the story, you can still hear the pain and emotion in his voice. As he got up off the hotel room floor and looked in the mirror, he didn't recognize himself. What he saw in the mirror looked more like the Devil than Larry Gatlin. He realized at that moment, at his absolute lowest, he had to do something to change his life. Over the following months and years, I watched my brother model six things that turned his greatest failure into his greatest success story: He *faced* it. He *fixed* it. He relied on his *faith*, *family*, and *friends*, because he chose to believe in his *future*.

Larry *faced* his struggle head-on. He had the courage and humility to stand up in front of people and say, "My name is Larry and I am an alcoholic and a drug addict"; not "I'm

Grammy-winning recording artist and multi-platinum song-writing celebrity Larry Gatlin—aren't you impressed?" Rather, Larry's simple acknowledgment of the humanness and less-than-perfect decision making we all share seemed to be a better place to start.

That's a pretty strong first step—admitting to ourselves and others that we have a problem. How about you—do you have problems in your life? How easy is it for you to admit that your life is not perfect and to share your struggles with others? If it is hard for you to admit that you have problems, you may wish to consider your thinking in this area.

Many people embrace what is called black-or-white or all-or-nothing thinking when it comes to their lives. Perhaps somewhere along the way you got the message that 1 percent bad equals all bad. This very common thinking pattern suggests that the bad in our lives wipes out the good. That's just faulty thinking. In truth, we all have good and bad parts, and the bad does not negate the good; they simply coexist. Do you allow yourself the grace to make mistakes?

It's interesting that many in the Christian faith are much harder on themselves than God appears to be, at least according to Scripture. Where in the Bible does it say that God holds us to a standard of perfection? Actually, Scripture teaches that "all have sinned and fall short of the glory of God" (Romans

3:23). In 1 John 1:8, it says, "If we claim to be without sin, we deceive ourselves and the truth is not in us."

Do you know that your mistakes, bad judgments, and sins cannot separate you from the love of God? Romans 8:38–39 says, "For I am convinced that neither death nor life, neither angels nor demons, neither the present nor the future, nor any powers, neither height nor depth, nor anything else in all creation, will be able to separate us from the love of God that is in Christ Jesus our Lord."

If you really want to make positive changes in your life, you have to face the truth that change is needed. Facing his addiction was my brother's turning point in becoming a sober man. It opened the door for him to find renewed passion and purpose in his life. When you stare your bad parts in the eye, you'll find they aren't as powerful as they seemed when you avoided them. What would you like to face? What's stopping you?

Larry's next step on his path to a new life was that he *fixed* it. He voluntarily admitted himself into a drug and alcohol rehabilitation center and submitted himself to their guidance and expertise. Surrounding himself with family and friends, he admitted his addiction to those who were closest to him, most of whom he'd lied to for years in an attempt to cover his tracks. He made restitution for his actions and asked for their forgiveness. These were family and friends he could count on for support and honesty. Larry has continued to pursue these relationships of loving accountability to this very day.

As Larry sought to fix his situation, he embraced an immutable truth we all must face as we seek to change: he couldn't do it alone. Neither can you. A good place to start your journey to lasting change is alongside others who are seeking the same. In Chapter 3 we touched on the importance of a healthy community of support. Even as he reengaged with the faith of his youth, Larry would not have made it had he tried to go it on his own. Having God as your only teammate is often a prescription for failure. We just aren't designed that way. Remember, it isn't God *or* people; it's God *and* people that are needed to live a life that embraces its full potential. Larry found a healing reflection of God's love and forgiveness in the caring embrace of his family and friends.

Larry's biggest failure turned into his greatest victory. Now, some thirty years later, he's still clean, and he's helped thousands of others in their quest for sobriety. Pretty cool, huh? Think about your biggest failures. Wouldn't it be awesome if they could become your greatest victories in life? They can! Don't take my word for it—ask my brother Larry.

It's important to grip the reality that wherever you find yourself today, your life is not over. Until you leave this life, you really do have possibility, but it's imperative to grasp this key concept: *failure is not final*. Many times because of our life experiences, we become discouraged and lose hope when we fail in the short term. Perhaps you've gotten messages somewhere along the way like "You'll never get that right," or "You're not good enough!" That's what happens when we are criticized. We begin to hear the critical voices in our head that suggest things will never work out for us. So parents, do you want your kids to succeed in life? Heap praise on them when they do something right and connect before you correct when they do something wrong. Your kids will then become *the little engine that could* instead of *the little engine that desperately wants to but is afraid to try*. Colossians 3:21 says, "Fathers, do not embitter your children, or they will become discouraged."

If you hear the discouraging thoughts that whisper you *cannot*, remind yourself that you are not defined by your short-term failures. As long as you have life, you can try again. It isn't over until *you* say it's over. Now, what do *you* say? Are you a created being? Were you created with a purpose and a plan? You'll have to decide what you believe about that for yourself. Clarifying your beliefs about why you're here, that is, why you exist, will help you move toward a life that is more genuine and purposeful.

Remember, you will not get it right every time. The best baseball players get only hits three out of ten tries. What are you to do when you miss the mark and disappoint yourself? *Get up.* And if you can't get up, spend what's left of your energy finding someone to help you get up. Continuing to doggedly pursue your passions, purpose, and what you perceive to be God's plan for your life will provide an education you cannot get anywhere else. *Your failures are not final—just fertilizer for your future success.*

The great inventor Thomas Edison was a great example of someone who viewed his many failures as fertilizer for his future success. In the early 1900s in the lab at his winter home in Fort Myers, Florida, he pushed his team to find a way to take the nickel-iron battery concept and make it practical for use in cars (so he could sell the batteries to his friend Henry Ford!). As the story goes, after more than five hundred experiments and a million dollars in expense, his assistants came to him and told him it could not be done. He is said to have replied, "Gentlemen, you now are armed with the knowledge of five hundred things which do not work—go find the one that does." After another four hundred or so experiments (and another million dollars), they finally found what they were looking for and soon recouped their money by selling the batteries to Henry Ford.

Like Thomas Edison, your failures contain great schooling in what does *not* work. You can spend your life being angry and bitter about your failures, or you can shift your focus to the lessons they teach. How we view our failures may very well shape our future. Consider this statement from arguably the best professional basketball player who ever lived, Michael Jordan: "I have missed more than nine thousand shots in my career. I have lost almost three hundred games. On twenty-six occasions I have been entrusted to take the game winning shot, and I missed. I have failed over and over and over again in my life. And that is why I succeed."

Another often-mentioned character in the "Failure Hall of Fame" is the sixteenth president of the United States, Abraham Lincoln. Any grade school student can tout the impact Lincoln had on this country and perhaps the entire world as he steadfastly stood strong for the dignity and worth of all men. His life, however, was dotted with far more failure than success. Consider Lincoln's path to finding his ultimate purpose:

- Lost his job, 1831
- Defeated for Illinois state legislature, 1832
- Failed in business, 1833
- Elected to Illinois state legislature, 1834
- Sweetheart (Ann Rutledge) died, 1835
- Had nervous breakdown, 1836
- Defeated for Illinois House Speaker, 1838

- Defeated for nomination for U.S. Congress, 1843
- Elected to U.S. Congress, 1846
- Lost renomination, 1848
- Rejected for Land Officer, 1849
- Defeated for U.S. Senate, 1854
- Defeated for nomination for vice president, 1856
- Again defeated for U.S. Senate, 1858
- Elected president, 1860

If you, like Edison, Jordan, and Lincoln, find your life has been dotted with more failure than success, you are in excellent company. Nearly all successful people find that the learning curve to achieving their dreams, goals, and purpose is fraught with frustrating failure. More examples:

- **Henry Ford**'s first two automobile companies failed. As history records, he persevered and changed the landscape of worldwide manufacturing when he was the first to apply assembly line production techniques. This process opened the door for the mass sales of affordable automobiles. He became one of the most famous and richest men in the world.

- **Steven Spielberg** ranks among the most successful and innovative filmmakers in history. During his childhood, Spielberg dropped out of junior high school. He was persuaded to come back and was placed in a learning-disabled class. While today Spielberg's name is synonymous with big budget, he was rejected three times from the University of Southern California School of Theater, Film, and Television.

- Author **J. K. Rowling** has made countless millions from her Harry Potter books and movies. It wasn't always that way. Before she published the series of novels, she was nearly penniless, severely depressed, divorced, and raising a child on her own while attending school and writing a novel. Rowling went from depending on welfare to being one of the richest women in the world in a span of only five years.

- Tennis player **Stan Smith** was rejected from even being a lowly ball boy for a Davis Cup tennis match because event organizers felt he was too clumsy and uncoordinated. Smith went on to prove them wrong, showcasing his not-so-clumsy skills by winning Wimbledon, the U. S. Open, and eight Davis Cups.

- You likely remember baseball legend **Babe Ruth** because of his long-standing home run record—a whopping 714 during his career! However, along with all those home runs came a pretty hefty number of strikeouts as well: 1,330! For several decades he held the all-time record for strikeouts. When asked about this, he simply said, "Every strike brings me closer to the next home run."

- **Ludwig van Beethoven**, the German composer of classical music, is widely regarded as a musical genius. Beethoven's early music teacher once said of him, "As a composer he is hopeless." Prior to penning some of his greatest works, he lost his hearing. Yes, a deaf man composed some of the world's most melodic and revered music.

- **Winston Churchill** failed the sixth grade. In later years he would point to that failure as a tipping point that inspired him to work harder. Ultimately he became the prime minister of the United Kingdom during World War II. Churchill is now regarded as one of the most important leaders in world history.

- **Albert Einstein** was a theoretical physicist who was commonly regarded as the most important scientist of the twentieth century. Among his many accolades and honors was the 1921 Nobel Prize for Physics. His early life gave no clue to the world-changing work he would accomplish later. When he was young his parents thought he was mentally retarded. His grades in school were so poor that a teacher asked him to quit, reportedly saying, "Einstein, you will never amount to anything!"

- In the twentieth century the Woolworth Company was a retail giant in America. It pioneered the concept of the "5 & 10 Cent Stores." The first Woolworth store was founded in 1878 by **Frank Winfield Woolworth**. Before starting his own business, Woolworth got a job in a dry goods store when he was twenty-one. According to legend, his employer would not let him serve any customer because Frank "didn't have enough common sense to serve the customers."

- **Isaac Newton** was perhaps the greatest English mathematician of his generation. His work on optics and gravitation made him one of the greatest scientists the world has known. He never did particularly well in school, and when put in charge of running the family farm, he failed miserably. He did so poorly that an uncle took charge and sent him off to Cambridge, where he finally blossomed into the scholar we know today.

- Most people are familiar with the large department store chain that bears his name, but **R. H. Macy** didn't always have it easy. He actually started seven failed businesses before finally hitting it big with his store in New York City.

- In 1947, one year into her contract, **Marilyn Monroe** was dropped by 20th Century Fox because her producer thought she was unattractive and could not act. Of course, she is now revered by the public as one of the twentieth century's most famous movie stars and pop icons. Decades after her death, her memorabilia still garners millions of dollars in sales annually.

- Most people know **Oprah Winfrey** as one of the most iconic faces on TV, as well as one of the richest and most successful women in the world. Things weren't always so good. Oprah endured a rough and often abusive childhood, as well as numerous career setbacks, including being fired from one job as a television reporter because she was, in the words of her boss, "unfit for TV."

- **John Grisham**'s first novel was rejected by sixteen agents and twelve publishing houses. Undeterred, he continued writing until he became a mega-successful author, mainly writing books about modern legal drama. He remains one of the best-selling novelists of today.

- **Bill Gates** didn't seem like a candidate for success after dropping out of Harvard and starting a failed first business called Traf-O-Data. While this early idea didn't work out, another Bill Gates idea fared remarkably better and became the global empire that is now Microsoft.

- The first time the young comedian **Jerry Seinfeld** performed at a comedy club, he looked out at the audience, froze, and was eventually jeered and booed off the stage. However, he went back the next night, completed his set to laughter and applause, and the rest is history.

- **Soichiro Honda** was turned down by Toyota Motor Corporation during a job interview for an engineering position. Unable to find work, he began to make motor scooters in his garage. Soon his neighbors began to buy them to navigate Japan's congested streets and his new company was born. Today, the Honda Motor Company has grown to become the world's largest motorcycle manufacturer and one of the most profitable automakers.

- In his first screen test, classic movie icon **Fred Astaire** did not impress. The testing director of MGM noted that Astaire, "Can't act, can't sing, [is] slightly bald, [and] can dance a little." Astaire went on to become an incredibly successful actor, singer, and dancer, and kept that note in his Beverly Hills home to remind him of where he came from.

- During his lifetime **Vincent van Gogh** sold only one painting, and that was to a friend for a very small amount of money. While van Gogh was never a success during his life, he methodically continued his painting, sometimes starving to complete his more than eight hundred known works. Today they are valued at hundreds of millions of dollars.

- **Charles Schultz**'s *Peanuts* comic strip has been a worldwide success since the 1950s, yet his high school yearbook staff rejected every single cartoon he submitted. In later life he was even turned down when he applied for a job with Walt Disney!

The list could go on, but suffice it to say that there is a common denominator among successful people—they have all failed. If you embrace the reality that failure isn't optional, that it happens to everyone, it becomes far less powerful. Realizing that everyone fails from time to time can help you understand that failure is actually part of the success process. Don't run from failure—embrace it.

Have you ever met people who have not tasted much failure, defeat, or trouble in their lives? Perhaps their parents or some other benefactor had the means to protect them from difficulty and bail them out of trouble every time. If you know peoplee who've led "charmed" (maybe *spoiled* is a better word) lives, how much character do they possess? Really, when have they had to learn to try hard and be courageous, steadfast, or faithful?

I've discovered that there are some good things that only suffering can bring, things like patience, courage, wisdom, maturity, and an ability to really understand others who are struggling. *Your failures are more than just an educational tool; they are the foundation on which your character is built.* Money and fame will come and go, but your character will stay with you for eternity. Perhaps that's what Rick Warren meant when he said that "God is more concerned with your character than your comfort" in his book *The Purpose Driven Life*. It is your character that will sustain you through the good and the tough times. Don't miss the growth and lessons you can learn from your failures—look for them and become the woman or man God intends you to be.

It's also important that as you seek to turn your failures into fertilizer for your future success *do not play the movie forward*. Do not put yourself in the impossible dilemma of trying to predict the outcome of your efforts. Looking too far down the road will cause discouragement and ultimate failure. The task looks too big and the mountain is too high. Just do what's in front of you. Small, measured changes are the key to long-term success. The Old Testament book of Job 8:7 says, "Your beginnings will seem humble, so prosperous will your future be."

You cannot predict the future, so stop trying. Seeking to control the future will keep you stuck and lead you to disaster. Ecclesiastes 8:7 says, "Since no one knows the future, who can tell someone else what is to come?" You do not have a reliable crystal ball, and gazing too far down the road will overwhelm you.

It's important to set a simple, sustainable structure. Very often our well-intended plans fail because we just make them too hard. As we begin to build our plans, adding layer after layer, it becomes an overwhelming mountain that keeps us from taking the first step. If you really want to change and turn your failures into success, you have to formulate a structure that involves simple, doable steps. There is an order to things in this world, and we see in Scripture that the steps have to be in order for them to succeed. The message of Proverbs 24:27 is, "Put your outdoor work in order and get your fields ready; after that, build your house."

Structure is essential, but far easier for some than others. Some people are very organized, while others struggle to find their keys and remember simple things on their to-do lists. Of course, some of that has to do with the individual ways our brains are wired and our life experiences. Perhaps you find yourself on the "Martha Stewart level" of organization and this is not an issue for you. But many of us are closer to the "Jerry Lewis movie" pandemonium end. Now I know some of you younger readers are thinking, *Who's Jerry Lewis?* (Again, look it up on the Internet—one of the most popular and funny movie actors of all time!)

Very often we put the cart before the horse when it comes to making changes, and we don't prepare in a manner that will support our ultimate success. So, for every area in which you'd like to change, here's the overriding principle: *when you don't possess the internal structure to do something, you must seek an external structure for support.* Just "willing yourself" to do better will not work. Set a simple structure for success, and if you can't, get help from someone who can. It is not a sin to need help—everyone does. Let's take a moment to review your road map to redeeming your failures:

- Set a small, simple, sustainable structure. Just do what's in front of you.

- Remember—your failures are not final.

- Do not predict the outcome; stay in the present.

- Look for help when you need it.

Our response to failure can very well set the course for our destiny. Consider the story of two of the most famous disciples of Jesus Christ: Peter and Judas. Both were part of the "inner circle" that traveled, ate, and interacted with the man Christians consider as God incarnate.

Let's start with Peter (then known as Simon). Jesus foresaw a great future for Simon, as recorded in Matthew 16:17–19: "Blessed are you, Simon son of Jonah, for this was not revealed to you by flesh and blood, but by my Father in heaven. And I tell you that you are Peter, and on this rock I will build my church, and the gates of Hades will not overcome it. I will give you the keys of the kingdom of heaven; whatever you bind on earth will be bound in heaven, and whatever you loose on earth will be loosed in heaven."

Wow—Jesus was telling Simon that the Christian church would be built around him and that he would be named Peter or Petra, which actually translates as "rock." Talk about pressure! The eternal future of millions would rest squarely on Peter's back. At the Last Supper Peter proudly pledged his undying loyalty to Jesus, as recorded in Luke 22:33: "Lord, I am ready to go with you to prison and to death." But it was not to be. The very next verse records Jesus's response: "I tell you, Peter, before the rooster crows today, you will deny three times that you know me."

Later, in Matthew 26:69–75, we see Jesus's dark prophecy unfold:

> Now Peter was sitting out in the courtyard, and a servant girl came to him. "You also were with Jesus of Galilee," she said. But he denied it before them all. "I don't know what you're talking about," he said. Then he went out to the gateway, where another servant girl saw him and said to the people there, "This fellow was with Jesus of Nazareth." He denied it again, with an oath: "I don't know the man!" After a little while, those standing there went up to Peter and said, "Surely you are one of them; your accent gives you away." Then he began to call down curses, and he swore to them, "I don't know the man!" Immediately a rooster crowed. Then Peter remembered the word Jesus had spoken: "Before the rooster crows, you will disown me three times." And he went outside and wept bitterly.

Despite his best intentions, Peter had failed. His fear for his own safety caused him to understandably react within his humanness. Realizing what he'd done, he felt great remorse. However, you'll recall that even prior to Peter's failure, Jesus had proclaimed him to be the rock upon which the Christian church would be built. In the midst of his pain and sorrow, how easy it would have been for Peter to forget that. He could have allowed his failure, his denial of Jesus, to be his life's epitaph—but he did not.

Peter went on to live another thirty-four years and saw, in his lifetime, the establishment of what we know today as the Christian church. As Peter embraced his failure, he seemingly found new resolve, determination, and purpose. In the months before he, like Christ, was publicly crucified, it is reported that Peter underwent horrific torture at the hands of his Roman guards. It is also reported that he led nearly fifty of them to a faith in Christ as Savior. Peter's failure was not final.

How different, though, is the story of another disciple of Christ, Judas. Judas betrayed Christ for thirty pieces of silver, which was given to him by the religious leaders of the day. Not unlike Peter, Judas was gripped with sorrow when he realized what he'd done. Matthew 27:3–5 tells the story: "When Judas, who had betrayed him, saw that Jesus was condemned, he was seized with remorse and returned the thirty pieces of silver to the chief priests and the elders. 'I have sinned,' he said, 'for I have betrayed innocent blood.' 'What is that to us?' they replied. 'That's your responsibility.' So Judas threw the money into the temple and left. Then he went away and hanged himself."

Both Peter and Judas failed and felt deep pangs of sorrow. Their response, however, could not have been more different. How they viewed their failures impacted their ultimate destinies. Clearly, Judas viewed his failure as final. He saw no hope, no future, and no way out. However, his thinking was simply not accurate. If Peter could be forgiven and find a purposeful life, why not Judas?

The central message of Christian belief is that we've all sinned and fallen short of God's perfect standard. Acknowledging and embracing our need for forgiveness opens the door for the future. Judas was halfway there—he acknowledged what he'd done was wrong and that he was sorry. He tried to make restitution as best he could by returning the blood money. But he could not do what Peter did: embrace forgiveness and move forward. Judas could not imagine God forgiving him and could not forgive himself. Apparently, Peter could.

How about you? You have made and will continue to make mistakes in life. Your failure is really only final if there's no forgiveness possible. How hard is it for you to embrace forgiveness? Perhaps it's easier for you to forgive others than to believe they could forgive you. When you don't believe forgiveness is possible, like Judas, it's easy to give up. I cannot say it any better than how Luke wrote in the book of Acts 13:38: "Therefore, my friends, I want you to know that through Jesus the forgiveness of sins is proclaimed to you."

As you seek to embrace and grow from your inevitable failures in life, ponder these questions:

- What has been my biggest failure?

- How has that failure impacted my life?

- What are the lessons I can glean from my failures?

- Where could I benefit from more structure in my life?

- Do I tend to try to predict the future and control the outcome of things?

- How easy is it for me to ask for help?

- How easy is it for me to forgive myself?

Chapter 6

SO:
SOLUTIONS
BEGIN
WITH ME

THROUGHOUT MY CAREER, one of the most challenging hurdles I've faced is the consistency level of on-site sound technicians who help me with my presentations. Because I sing during my speeches, good audio support is essential. In a perfect world, I would always take an audio person with me, but that just doesn't make sense for a variety of reasons, so I usually find myself at the mercy of whoever is there. Sometimes it's a great production company, and sometimes it's been the janitor—literally! Luckily for me, that janitor happened to know his stuff and all went well.

I always do a sound check at least an hour before my presentations. And in an attempt to cover all my bases, I always phone ahead a month in advance to speak with the person assigned to run the sound and lighting. On one occasion I spoke with a lovely lady named Rhonda who assured me she had my needs covered for the upcoming program. As always, I arrived with cautious optimism an hour before start time to check the sound. The venue was a gorgeous theater, beautifully decorated for Christmas, complete with an amazing audio and lighting system. I was pleasantly surprised to say the least. However, all of Rhonda's controls were backstage—not the best location for audio and lighting cues. From backstage you can't really hear and see what the audience does.

I could tell right away, though, that Rhonda really knew her stuff. I gave her my script and she began to go through my song accompaniment tracks, making notes on the audio levels of each one to ensure consistency. As I said, she was working from *behind* the curtain, but instead of complaining about the less-than-optimal location, she walked out into the audience area during the sound check to make sure the levels were just right. She asked me if I would mind singing each song through completely so she could hear the nuances within them and make notes on audio as well as lighting cues. I was so grateful for her attention to detail, but I didn't truly realize the power of her commitment to excellence until the actual performance.

When the curtain went up and it was showtime, Rhonda was nothing short of amazing. She never missed a cue. Not only did she adjust the lighting to fit the mood of the song, she tweaked it within the song. When the lyric became more intimate, when I sang a bit softer, she would reduce the lighting or add more blue hues, tiny little things that made a *huge* difference in the experience to the audience. Interestingly enough, these tiny changes had the most profound effect on *me*. As I was singing, I noticed her "little tweaks," and guess what happened? I *sang better!* Her commitment to excellence made me a better performer, and everyone benefited!

At the end of my performance, the emcee came back onstage to thank me. But before she could say a word, I brought Rhonda out to center stage and told the audience that this gifted lady was the one who had made our last hour together so special. I explained that because of her amazing talent, I could totally relax. I just had to stand up there and sing and talk.

Clearly, this was not Rhonda's comfort zone. She'd spent her entire career behind the curtain, so to be singled out for public acknowledgment and praise was foreign territory. I didn't want to make her uncomfortable, but I felt compelled to honor her efforts. Letting her go unnoticed seemed to be unjust. The crowd went wild and enthusiastically applauded this dedicated lady.

Afterward Rhonda told me that that was the first time in twenty-nine years of facilitating artists' performances that she'd ever been brought onstage and publicly acknowledged. Can you imagine that?

This lady took her job seriously and went about her business skillfully, never expecting anything in return, save the sheer enjoyment of practicing her craft. She knew that her abilities would make the performance stronger, and she quietly, skill-fully did her thing. Interestingly, I received many compliments from the audience for my performance that day. But the phrase I heard most often was, "Thank you for recognizing Rhonda; that was *so* special."

Each of us has abilities within us that can help our fellow man. Yet too often, our human nature (or fear!) prohibits us from getting involved. Have you ever heard the story about the person who fell into a ditch? Several different people walked by and had their own idea about how to help this individual.

- The *sympathetic person* walked by and said, "Oh, I really feel for you in that ditch."

- The *objective person* walked by and said, "You know, it makes perfect sense that someone would fall into that ditch."

- The *mathematician* walked by and calculated the exact size of the ditch.

- The *news reporter* walked by and asked for the exclusive story on the ditch.

- The *IRS agent* walked by and said, "Hey buddy, are you paying taxes on that ditch?"

- Then the *preacher* walked by and said, "Your sins have put you in the ditch."

- The *psychiatrist* walked by and said, "No, your parents have put you in the ditch!"

- The *optimist* walked by and said, "Things could get a lot worse."

- The *pessimist* walked by and said, "Things will get a lot worse!"

What if you walked by and saw someone in that ditch? What would *your* response be? What if you simply reached out your hand and said, "Here, take my hand and let me see if I can help you out of the ditch." Sometimes the most sensible solution is right in front of us—it just involves putting our needs and agenda behind another's. Many times a selfless *action* is the key to a lasting solution.

Other times it's a change in *attitude* that's required. It's remarkable how options and solutions seem to fall into place when we confront our struggles with a change in attitude. How we frame our thoughts affects our feelings and actions. Considering that there may be a different point of view or perspective often opens the door for productive solutions.

For example, which statement feels more like it might lend itself to a solution: *I know I'm right* or *What do you think? I deserve this* or *I'm very grateful?* Attitude can make a huge difference when it comes to finding the most helpful solutions, as illustrated by this story:

Two battleships had been on training maneuvers in heavy weather for several days, and the captain stayed on the bridge because he wanted to be aware of any changes in the raging seas. Suddenly, a report came: "Captain, a light is bearing on the starboard bow." "Is she steady or moving astern?" asked the captain. The lookout replied, "She's steady, Captain," which meant they were on a collision course with the other ship. The captain said to the signal man, "Signal that ship: 'We are on a collision course. I advise you to change your course twenty degrees.'" In a few seconds, back came the flashing signal reply: "Advise you change your course twenty degrees." The captain dusted off his medals, stood a bit more erect, looked at the signal man, and said, "Signal that ship: 'I am a captain and I advise you change *your* course twenty degrees.'" Again, in a few seconds, back came the flashing reply: "I am a seaman, second class, and I advise you to change *your* course twenty degrees." The captain was totally miffed by now and spat out the final order, shouting to his signal man, "Signal that ship: 'I am a battleship and I advise you change your course twenty degrees now!'" Finally, back came the final flashing signal: "I, sir, am a lighthouse." The captain changed his attitude—and his course.

Solutions often begin with you, an action you can take or an attitude you can change. As we've addressed previously, there are very few things outside of your own actions and attitude that are in your control, but you do have a large measure of influence over certain parts of your life. I would even go so far as to suggest that you have a responsibility to develop the skills, patience, and wisdom to know when to act—and when to step back.

In some sense that's the tightrope we all walk—when to seek to impose our will and when to submit to God's will. Of course, if you don't believe in God, you're pretty much on your own and have to find your way yourself. But if you're willing to consider that there may be a higher power, justice, and plan than that which you can see through your eyes alone, you may want to consider what is—and what is not—your responsibility.

From the Christian faith perspective, we clearly see that there are times when we are best served by submitting our actions and attitudes to God. Even Jesus submitted his will to his Heavenly Father's when facing death by crucifixion. Matthew 26:42 says, "He [Jesus] went away again a second time and prayed, saying, 'My Father, if this cannot pass away unless I drink it, your will be done (NASB).'"

It is, however, difficult to submit your life, will, actions, attitude, pain, past, and purpose to God's will unless you first own them yourself. You can't give away something you don't own. Who owns your life? Who should control it? Many of us feel our lives, in general, are very much out of control—out of our control, out of God's control, just spinning wildly through eternity. Others have a heightened need to control everything—our lives and the lives of everyone around us. We rely on the feeling that if we can maintain control (or at least the illusion of it), nothing bad will happen, as if God leaves it *all* up to us. That's a lot of pressure for a human.

Unfortunately, we often move toward the polar ends of the "control" spectrum. On one end, we are powerless to stop the stuff that happens to us, while on the other end, we must assume 100 percent responsibility for life. Neither scenario paints a very pretty picture. Who's in charge—us or God? Can it be both? Let's look at it the following way.

Ultimately, we all must submit to the reality that we are not God and are not totally in charge. However, the Christian perspective concerning God's grace does allow us to be in charge of that which is within the scope of our capability. In other words, God gave you certain ownership responsibilities, kind of like when you lease a car—you are still responsible for oil changes, putting gas in, paying the insurance, driving within the limits of the law, having a valid driver's license, and making the payments. If you don't do those things, it's your fault and you reap the consequences.

Owning your life is, in some sense, accepting control or ownership of what God has given you to use: your free will, brain, his support system of people, and the simple gift of choice. As an adult you have the capacity to choose. Some of us just never learned how to do that well. When you use your adult voice and exercise your adult choices, you'll find that solutions to your struggles will tend to follow. I believe God has a purpose for assigning us ownership responsibilities for our lives. He is preparing us for service, to know him, to experience life (good and bad), to grow our perspective, and ultimately experience heaven.

It is not unlike requiring a child to walk. If the child doesn't, her muscles atrophy and become useless. She is unable to care for herself or anyone else. By allowing, encouraging, and even forcing her to walk badly, stumble, and wobble, you equip her to eventually run.

God would not cheat us by doing everything for us and crippling our quest to fulfill our passions and his purpose for our lives. God has no desire to spoil us. Think of what spoiled kids turn into—characterless, miserable adults who are unable to see other people's perspectives or deal with life on any terms other than their own. Nobody likes them, no one respects them, and few ever learn to love them.

You are in charge of many parts of your life, but not *all* the parts of your life. The key is identifying and owning your part. God gave you the legs—you have to use them to learn to walk. As a child, you are powerless to make certain choices that could protect you and help you move forward. You really do have limited control over certain circumstances. Here's the good news: you are not a kid anymore.

Are you holding on to a childlike stance of powerlessness because it's what you know and have grown comfortable with? Perhaps it feels safe and you wouldn't know how to live otherwise. One reason we hold on to that childlike stance is because we're still holding out for justice to prevail and for all past wrongs to be made right. If you spend your life, energy, and time trying to right past wrongs, you will be frustrated and ill-equipped to invest your heart and energies in productive efforts. The Bible does proclaim, however, that justice will ultimately prevail. Here are some scriptural promises:

- Isaiah 25:8: "He will swallow up death forever.
  The Sovereign LORD will wipe away the tears

from all faces; he will remove the disgrace of his
people from all the earth. The LORD has spoken."

- Revelation 7:17: "For the Lamb at the center of
the throne will be their shepherd; he will lead
them to springs of living water. And God will
wipe away every tear from their eyes."

- Revelation 21:4: "He will wipe every tear from
their eyes. There will be no more death or
mourning or crying or pain, for the old order of
things has passed away."

All of these promises are about eternity. Until then, God's
grace, which gives us free will and choice, has left us to play the
cards we're dealt. So, one of the great questions of life is *What
are you going to do with what you have?*

- Spouse cheated? *What are you going to do with
what you have?*

- Parents hurt you? *What are you going to do with
what you have?*

- Health failing? *What are you going to do with
what you have?*

- Depressed and anxious? *What are you going to do with what you have?*

- Disappointed with life? *What are you going to do with what you have?*

How will you respond to life's ups and downs? Taking charge of your life is all about *your* response. If it's all about what *others* do, they own you and you're in a hopeless, powerless position. Perhaps, like Dorothy in *The Wizard of Oz*, you've always had the power to go back to Kansas but didn't know how to use it or were afraid. You might not want to leave your one dependable, consistent, comfort-zone friend—your pain. Pain can become your friend. Unfortunately, pain is a friend that takes and does not give much back.

As adults we can learn to respond well to even the most painful situations instead of doing what many of us have learned to do—surrender our power and control to the more comfortable *victim* position. On some level, we all belong to the "Dr Pepper song" victim club: "I'm a victim, you're a victim, she's a victim, he's a victim, wouldn't you like to be a victim too?" Granted, you may have been a legitimate victim of horrific actions by someone or circumstances beyond your control. Remember, a victim may very well be *what* you are, but it does not have to be *who* you are.

It's easy to enroll in the victim club because we've all faced injustice at some point in our lives. For comfort and support, there is always a throng of fellow victims longing to ease the shared pain by connecting with you in a giant circle of misery. It feels temporarily good and supportive, but it is not helpful. More than that, it does *nothing* to change your situation. Stewing about the unfairness of life keeps us stuck in the mud field of wishing things were different instead of embracing what is. Remember, *when you argue with reality, you lose 100 percent of the time.* What makes it so hard to accept life's tough parts?

For one thing, in America we seem to think we have the right to be happy—all the time! Even the U.S. Constitution does not guarantee that; it only acknowledges that we should have the right to *the pursuit of happiness.* How realistic is it to think that life will always be fair and just? It won't be. Everyone is a victim at times, and accepting that will help you own your part in finding helpful solutions that are healing.

I'll give you another example of how a solution can begin with you. A couple I know is continually at odds over finances. He feels she spends too much and that she doesn't appreciate the burden he feels being the primary financial provider. She feels unloved and demeaned when he challenges her spending habits. They both feel they're treated unjustly; they blame each other and feel the situation would be fine if the other person's behavior would change. But because they couldn't really change the other person, they felt stuck and hopeless, and their marriage was drifting into isolation.

I suggested they change their response in this way: instead of focusing on the other person's behavior, focus on how that behavior makes you feel and communicate that. Now they were not blaming but sharing and owning their own issue and perspective. You'd be amazed at how empowering this is. It can help you get unstuck and move you to fruitful action. Instead of wondering why she needed so much money to go to the store, I recommended they go to the store together, so he could appreciate what things really cost and feel part of the decision process. Likewise, I asked her to sit with him and pay the bills for a few months to get a better perspective on where the money went, so that she would feel like she had a voice in the decisions.

After a period of time they both left the fruitless blame-excuse game behind and focused on reality and actual, not imagined, responsibilities. As they changed their focus to their own actions and feelings, the healing began. Their actions to proactively participate in understanding the other's perspective felt more like their own choice, not a forced response. It was now their shared issue, not just the other person's fault.

When you start owning your part, hope comes to life. The truth is even in the most unjust situations, where you had little or no choice and were hurt beyond imagination, the question remains the same: *what are you going to do with what you have?* Try this . . .

- Focus on what *is* instead of what *should* be.
- Focus on what you *can* do, not what you *can't*.
- Focus on your behavior; not on others' behavior.

As you begin to own your life, you also begin to discover that you are a lot richer than you thought. You discover God's wonderful gift of an adult choice and an adult voice. You have more freedom and power to respond than you might think. What can happen is that we become conditioned to feel inaction is our only choice. Any circus trainer will tell you that repeated and familiar conditioning of wild animals is the key to controlling their behavior. If a circus elephant is chained to a certain location for any length of time, they begin to believe they are destined to stay put. After a period of time the trainer no longer has to chain the elephant. It just stays where it thinks it is stuck with no chains.

Are you at all like the circus elephant in certain areas of your life? Have you become so used to the "chains" of your situation that you are afraid to move, even when the chains are no longer there? Perhaps you have been chained to the fence so long you won't move, even though the chains are broken. The chains are off—you can move, you have choices about your response to life. Just take the first step and others will follow.

Once you've determined that you do, in fact, have the ability to change your actions and attitude, you have taken the first step in discovering your purpose and God's plan for your life. Yes, one person really can make a difference. History books are filled with true stories of simple people who found they had the capacity to change their lives and in turn affect many others. Consider these who found that solutions began with them:

- **Mother Teresa** attained worldwide fame for her life dedicated to serving the poor and destitute in the slums of Calcutta.

- British statesman **William Wilberforce** fought tirelessly to end the slave trade in his native England. He once said, "God Almighty has set before me two great objects, the suppression of the slave trade and the reformation of morality."

- Heralded as the founder of modern nursing, **Florence Nightingale** helped to revolutionize the treatment of patients after her experience of treating wounded soldiers in the Crimean War.

- **Anne Frank** was just an ordinary teenage girl, but she became a symbol of how ordinary people can get caught up in man's inhumanity. Her diary, written during the Holocaust, is an amazing testament to the power of the human spirit in the face of evil.

- At a time when racism reached a fever pitch in worldwide politics, African American track athlete **Jesse Owens** won four gold medals at Hitler's 1936 Olympics in Berlin. Hitler left his chancellor's box seat during Owens's medal presentation ceremonies as the world watched one man single-handedly puncture the Nazi ideology of Aryan supremacy.

- With the dreaded disease of polio affecting millions around the world, **Dr. Jonas Salk** discovered and developed the first safe and effective polio vaccine.

While you may not invent a cure for a disease or do something that impacts millions, do not be quick to discount the power of your personal actions. Whether you recognize it or not, you are affecting the lives of those around you. Your words, actions, and attitudes have tremendous power. How will you choose to use them in the days ahead? Here's a little experiment you can try that illustrates this point.

The next three times you check out at the grocery store, respond to the cashier with a flat expression on your face and a minimum of words. When they greet you with something along the lines of "Did you find everything okay?" give them an expressionless "Uh huh" and take note of their reaction. The next three times, begin your interchange with a smile on your face and respond more enthusiastically, like, "I sure did—and thanks so much for asking!" Check out their response to that. I guarantee it will be different. If you can impact a stranger with a change in your attitude and actions, imagine what you could do within your family and circle of friends. Do you want your life to make a difference for those you care about? Consider the power of the simple interactions you have every day.

Who has changed your life with their words and actions? Almost assuredly your parents did. How about a teacher, coach, clergyperson, or trusted friend? Recognizing that what you do and say has a powerful impact on others is helpful in understanding your true value as a person. How do you view yourself? As unique, capable, and worthy, or perhaps as something less than that? Maybe you view yourself as basically defective, with little to offer to others and society in general.

If solutions are truly to begin with you, it's important to embrace your value as a person, and that can be difficult if you've become convinced you're not valuable. If this is how you feel at times, you may wish to consider where that message came from. What happened in your life that led you to the conclusion that you are not good enough to make a difference for yourself and others?

What do you believe makes a person valuable? What they do or have done? Their intellect? How much money they have? Their status in society? Kindness, honesty, integrity, generosity, or business acumen? How do you assign worth to people? It's a good idea to get that settled in your mind and heart, because how you assign worth to other people is essentially how you assign value to yourself.

In the 1990s Dr. Marino traveled extensively in the former Soviet-bloc countries in Eastern Europe. He observed that two generations of communist rule had left the citizenry with the idea that their value as people was based on their value to the state. If they were a champion athlete or brilliant scientist who could serve the state well, they had more value. Those with more state-serving value lived in nicer housing, ate better, and looked down upon those whom the state classified as ordinary. That, however, is the opposite of the scriptural picture of human value. The Bible teaches that the ground is level in God's view. Romans 3:23 says that "all have sinned and fall short of the glory of God." In a sense, it's saying that no one has value over another and that we all have equal God-given value.

Is your value based on what you've done or who you are? Certainly, you should be proud of your accomplishments, but accomplishments alone will leave you in a state of constant striving, seeking to find your worth in the next achievement. You will get tired sooner than later.

How do you see yourself? Are you a creation of God, loved unconditionally despite what you have or haven't accomplished? That can be tough in America because it seems we're terribly consumed by what we do. Soon after you meet someone the inevitable question will pop up, "So, what do you do?" We seem to place a higher value on what we do than who we are. Dr. Marino relates that he often asks his counseling clients to tell him about the "good parts" of themselves. Most often they say things like, "I'm a regular church attender, I take good care of my family, and I volunteer at the soup kitchen." Rarely do they say things like, "I'm smart, attractive, funny, and kind." See the difference? Our focus is often on our actions instead of our personhood. Yes, good and right actions are important, but in the long run they stem from who we are.

Who are you? If solutions truly start with you, that's a question you'll need to begin to answer. Take a few minutes to do an honest self-examination.

- What are the good parts of me?

- What parts could I use some work on?

- Who has really impacted my life? How?

- Whose life have I impacted? How?

- How much time do I spend focusing on past events that cannot be changed?

- When have I been a legitimate victim of something hurtful?

- In what areas of my life could I do a better job of "owning" my part?

- In what areas of my life could I do a better job of releasing responsibility for things over which I have no control?

- Whom could I impact with a kind word or action today?

Chapter 7

LA:
LAUGH

A JOYFUL HEART IS GOOD MEDICINE, but a broken spirit dries up the bones" (Prov. 17:22 NASB). Ain't it the truth! God knows we have enough stress in our lives today. All the modern conveniences that were supposed to make our lives simpler . . . what happened there?

Do you have stress in your life? Hold a mirror up to your mouth. If it fogs up when you breathe on it, I'm certain you do! Even modern medicine has begun to tout the health benefits of laughter. If you keep your eyes open, you'll discover that life is full of funny moments.

If you have children, you won't have to look too hard to find the laughter. With a wonderful innocence, kids call it like they see it. I remember taking my then three-year-old son, Caleb, to the department store. He was a typical three-year-old and did *not* want to be in the china department of Macy's, but I was desperate to get a wedding gift I'd put off buying. Suffice it to say, the china department and my son weren't extremely compatible. This was about the same time as the first *Star Wars* movie had been released and Caleb loved it; he thought he *was* Hans Solo. Finally, I found what I was looking for and sat him on the counter as I checked out. As I did so, I noticed that the sales associate, who'd been so kind to put up with my *wild child*, had a beautiful brooch pinned on her lapel. I commented on how pretty it was. She explained to me that it was a family heirloom and had been passed down to her from her great-grandmother. She hoped to give it to her daughter in the future. I thought, *What a lovely idea*, but out of the corner of my eye, I could see that Caleb was paying very close attention to this conversation.

In his three-year-old mind he was thinking, *Mommy said something nice to this lady, so I think I'll say something nice to this lady.* If you're a parent, my guess is you've been there. You know your child is going to say something, and it's not going to be good. A warning tingle starts at the base of your spine and makes its way up your back until the hair stands up on your neck. You know they're going to say it, and here it comes! My son proceeded to say what is possibly the most politically incorrect statement ever uttered on planet Earth when he looked at this dear lady and said for all of Macy's to hear, "Lady, I like your boobies!"

I turned at least seven shades of red. I prayed for God to strike me dead. I prayed for a giant hole in the earth to swallow me up. When none of those things happened, my sense of humor kicked in and I said, "What can I say; he's just like his father!" Do you know what that lady did? She laughed! Thank goodness she laughed; I suppose she could have sued me! We laughed loud and long—it felt great to just let go.

When was the last time you really laughed? I've spoken with people who truly can't remember a time in their life when laughter was at least a part of their day. That's what the overwhelming pace, stress, and sadness of our modern world can do to you. It creeps into your life slowly, and before you know it, it takes over.

If you're not experiencing any joy in your life, that's somewhat like when the CHECK ENGINE light starts flashing on your car's dashboard. Something's going on and it's time for an emotional tune-up. In fact, one of the diagnostic criteria for clinical depression is a condition called *anhedonia*. Anhedonia is the opposite of hedonism. It's an emotional state that leaves you incapable of experiencing pleasure. In lay terms, it's an extremely pessimistic view of life.

Interestingly, people who have difficulty experiencing joy or pleasure in life are often plagued by a variety of physical maladies. It does seem that science continues to reveal a strong link between our emotional and physical health. The emotional, physical, and helping virtues of laughter have sparked many memorable quotes, such as these:

- *Laughter is a tranquilizer with no side effects.*
  —Humorist Arnold Glasow

- *With the fearful strain that is on me night and day, if I did not laugh I should die.*
  —President Abraham Lincoln

- *Man, when you lose your laugh you lose your footing.*
  —Author Ken Kesey

- *Seven days without laughter makes one weak.*
  —American cartoonist Mort Walker

- *I am thankful for laughter, except when milk comes out of my nose.*
  —Actor/director Woody Allen

- *A happy heart makes the face cheerful, but heartache crushes the spirit.*
  —Proverbs 15:13

- *Even if there is nothing to laugh about, laugh on credit.*
  —Author Unknown

- *Mirth is God's medicine. Everybody ought to bathe in it.*
  —Preacher/abolitionist Henry Ward Beecher

- *The most wasted of all days is that in which we have not laughed.*
  —Writer Nicolas Chamfort

- *Laughter is an instant vacation.*
  —Comedian Milton Berle

- *So many tangles in life are ultimately hopeless that we have no appropriate sword other than laughter.*
  —Psychologist Gordon W. Allport

- *Laughter is the shortest distance between two people.*
  —Comedian Victor Borge

- *What soap is to the body, laughter is to the soul.*
  —Yiddish Proverb

- *When people are laughing, they're generally not killing each other.*
  —Actor Alan Alda

- *Laughter and tears are both responses to frustration and exhaustion. I myself prefer to laugh, since there is less cleaning up to do afterward.*
  —Writer Kurt Vonnegut

- *A good laugh and a long sleep are the best cures in the doctor's book.*
  —Old Irish Proverb

- *Laughter gives us distance. It allows us to step back from an event, deal with it and then move on.*
  —Comedian Bob Newhart

- *I've always thought that a big laugh is a really loud noise from the soul saying "Ain't that the truth."*
  —Music impresario Quincy Jones

- *Laughter is the corrective force which prevents us from becoming cranks.*
  —Philosopher Henri Bergson

- *Remember, men need laughter sometimes more than food.*
  —Author Annie Fellows Johnston

- *A good time to laugh is any time you can.*
  —TV personality Linda Ellerbee

- *Laughter is the sun that drives winter from the human face.*
  —Poet and writer Victor Hugo

- *A man isn't poor if he can still laugh.*
  —American actor Raymond Hitchcock

Just how healing is laughter? From a purely biological perspective, the growing mountain of evidence suggests it is as helpful as eating well and exercising. An interesting study was presented at the European Society of Cardiology Congress in Paris on August 28, 2011 (see http://spo.escardio.org/eSlides/view.aspx?ccvtid=48&fp=351 to read the entire article). It showed that laughter really is good medicine. Researchers discovered that watching a movie that produces laughter can lead to blood vessel expansion similar to what you might experience with aerobic exercise, and the opposite of that was observed after watching a movie that caused mental stress.

In the study, three hundred participants watched segments of a funny movie, *There's Something about Mary*, on one day and on another day they watched the violent opening segment of the World War II movie *Saving Private Ryan*. The results showed a 30–50 percent difference in blood vessel diameter between the laughter and mental stress phases caused by the two movies.

Dr. Michael Miller, the lead researcher, noted, "The magnitude of change we saw in the endothelium [or inner cell wall of a blood vessel] after laughing was consistent and similar to the benefit we might see with aerobic exercise or statin drug use." He continued, "The endothelium is the first line in the development of atherosclerosis or hardening of the arteries, so it is very possible that laughing on a regular basis may be useful to incorporate as part of an overall healthy lifestyle to prevent heart disease." In other words, eat your veggies, exercise, and get a good belly laugh every day!

There is very little bad news about laughter. Of course, the ill-timed, insensitive laugh can make for an awkward moment, but for the most part, laughter is a God-given agent of healing.

- It has *social benefits*. It builds relationships, makes us more attractive, promotes emotional bonding, and helps diffuse conflict.

- It has *psychological benefits*. Laughter eases anxiety and fear. It relieves stress and improves mood. It has even been shown that people who laugh on a regular basis have a better ability to rebound from loss and discouragement.

- And beyond the blood flow positives mentioned above, laughter has other remarkable *physical benefits*. It is used to treat chronic pain and as a relaxation therapy tool. It also appears to reduce the production of stress hormones, which in turn boosts your immune system.

Given that we've established that laughter is a good thing, let me ask this question: are you having any fun? Remember the song of that same title popularized in 1958 when Tony Bennett recorded it with the Count Basie Orchestra? In 1958 we still knew how to have fun, or at least our idea of what *was* fun included taking an occasional break from life's tough parts. People would go for leisurely "Sunday drives" and sit (in their cars!) through a cartoon and a "double-feature" of two monster movies at the local drive-in theater. High-brow and sophisticated? No, but it did provide a respite from the drama. Today we seem to run from crisis to crisis, chased by the latest electronic device in our pocket. We were not designed to go all out all the time. Even God rested on the seventh day when creating the universe.

When was the last time you took a break from the drama? Drama can become addictive. There's a reason that reality TV shows filled with conflict and drama are so popular. Other people's pain has, in a sense, become our entertainment. If just hearing the word *drama* sends familiar tingles up your spine, I can tell you this: you'd feel much better if you surrendered your addiction to drama. Chaos, confusion, and commotion can become a familiar and habitual way of life. It's easy to become dependent on an uproar-dominated lifestyle filled with turbulence and mayhem.

What? Why would anyone willingly embrace that? Well, it could be that this "soap opera" existence has become your comfort zone and feels normal to you. Drama becomes your friend because it keeps you from having to embrace your real and sometimes very painful issues! Sitting in the quiet calm with your true feelings and emotions can be scary. It's sometimes easier to put on the "mask" of busyness, problem solving, and crisis management, so you can hide.

If you're hiding from the good parts of life, stop it! Of course, that's easier to say than do; this is a difficult world and these are difficult days to live in. Where do you find little islands of joy in your life? If you don't have them, perhaps it's time to start looking. What do you enjoy doing? What activities spell f-u-n for you? Clarifying your thinking about this will act as an emotional GPS system to point you in the right direction. Very often we spend our time, energy, and resources engaging in activities that we don't particularly enjoy. If you don't *have* to do it and you don't *like* it, *stop* it! You have a choice about where you invest your life. An occasional oasis of self-indulgent pleasure is not going to hurt anyone. In fact, it will refresh and energize you on every level. Being kind to yourself is not a sin.

The whole concept of having choices in life is foreign to many of us. Do you ever feel "trapped" by your circumstances? On some level, adult responsibilities do cause us to face our obligations. We are, in a sense, trapped by the realities of adult life. We are not, however, sentenced to a never-ending prison term of selfless service. If we embrace that posture, one where our needs are continually placed behind everything else in the world, we become exhausted, bitter, and ineffective in every area of life. It's not the way we were designed.

Are you weary of life? Burnout among Americans is perhaps at an all-time high, with economic and social pressures closing in on all fronts. In 1900 the average American slept nine hours every night—today we sleep about six. Even if you believe in evolution, we wouldn't evolve that quickly. One of the key brain chemicals that regulates mood is called serotonin. Proper levels of serotonin help keep us from getting too depressed or anxious. Most of the serotonin in your brain is manufactured while you sleep. If you're sleep-deprived, you're likely serotonin-deprived as well.

If you're not sleeping well or enough, why? What's getting in the way of a good night's rest for you? Fixing that issue may open the door for much more joy in your life. There are a multitude of safe and effective natural sleep aids, as well as others prescribed by physicians. Here are some of the most-common sleep wreckers . . .

- **Pets in bed:** Lots of people let their pets snuggle in bed with them for comfort, but evidence suggests that animals in bed make it harder to sleep. According to a survey done at the Mayo Clinic Sleep Disorders Center, 53 percent of people who sleep with pets say that their animals disturb their sleep. Animals don't have the same sleep and wake cycles that we do. If you're feeling chronically exhausted, take a break from the multispecies slumber parties and see if it makes a difference with your disturbed sleep.

- **Alcohol:** While drinking may make some people drowsy, alcohol typically disrupts the body's natural sleep patterns. Even though it may act as a sedative initially, it tends to signal your brain to wake up as the blood alcohol level drops. Most physicians recommend abstaining from alcohol two to three hours before bedtime to avoid sleep disruption.

- **Medicine, vitamins, and supplements:** Some common causes of disturbed sleep may be in your medicine cabinet. Steroids for asthma and beta-blockers for high blood pressure or heart problems can keep you up at night. Certain supplements can also cause sleep loss, like ginseng and guarana, which are stimulants. Even vitamins aren't free of sleep risk. Vitamins B_6 and B_{12} have been associated with vivid dreams, which can wake you up. If chronic sleep problems are part of your life, be sure to ask your physician if all the medicines, vitamins, and supplements could be causing your sleep issues.

- **Pain:** Even mild pain can cause disrupted sleep. Headaches, back pain, arthritis, and menstrual pain are all common causes, and they don't even have to wake you up. Pain signals sent out by your body can fragment your sleep, reducing the amount of time you spend in deep, restorative sleep.

What can you do to have a better night's sleep? Here are some of the most common physician recommendations:

- **Make the room dark.** Sleep studies have shown that the darker it is, the better you'll sleep. Use heavy curtains or shades to block light from windows or try an eye mask to cover your eyes.

- **Keep your room cool.** The temperature of your bedroom affects your sleep. Most people sleep better in a slightly cool room (around 65° F) with adequate ventilation. A bedroom that is too hot or too cold can interfere with quality sleep.

- **Keep the noise down**. While it may not be realistic to avoid all noise, you can attempt to mask it with a fan, recorded soothing sounds, or white noise. You can buy special sound machines that produce those noises or generate your own white noise by setting your radio between stations. Earplugs may also be a good option.

- **Make sure your bed is comfortable.** You should have enough room to stretch and turn comfortably. If you often wake up with a sore back or neck, you may wish to consider a new mattress or a different pillow.

- **Stay away from big meals at night.** Avoid heavy, rich foods within two hours of bed. Fat-laden foods are more difficult for your stomach to digest and may keep you up. Also, spicy or acidic foods can cause stomach issues and disrupt natural sleep patterns.

- **Turn off your television and computer.** Many people use the television to fall asleep or relax at the end of the day. Actually, the light suppresses melatonin production, which is helpful for sleep. Television also tends to stimulate the mind, not relax it.

- **Cut down on caffeine.** You may be surprised to learn that caffeine can cause sleep problems up to twelve hours after drinking it! If sleep is an issue for you, try losing the caffeine after lunch.

- **Try to make relaxation your goal, not sleep.** When sleep is not coming easily, don't try too hard. Try relaxation techniques such as deep breathing, prayer/meditation, or Scripture reading. While not a replacement for sleep, rest and relaxation still help rejuvenate your body.

WHAT ABOUT YOUR WORK— DOES IT BRING YOU ANY JOY?

You've likely heard people say, "I hate my job!" Perhaps those very words have trickled from your mouth at times. Certainly, there are few jobs that are fun all the time, but having a sense of purpose and mission in your work can make your chosen vocation a vacation. The popular business leadership thinking of our day is that the ultimate goals of any enterprise are best served when you have the right people in the right jobs. In his popular business book *Good to Great,* author Jim Collins speaks frequently about the value of having *the right people in the right seats on the bus.*

Is what you do a good fit for your desires, talents, and temperament? We all have certain God-given aptitudes, which Scripture confirms in Romans 12:6: "We have different gifts, according to the grace given to each of us." Finding a match for something you're good at and truly enjoy is often a great clue in the search for your ultimate purpose and God's plan for your life.

Some years ago Pastor Rick Warren of Saddleback Church in California developed the S.H.A.P.E. test, which is an acronym for Spiritual gifts, Heart, Abilities, Personality, and Experience. The test measures a variety of highly personalized traits to best match the user's desires and abilities. Doing an honest personal and spiritual inventory, such as the S.H.A.P.E. test, can help you discover joy in your life.

Think about it: whether you are a corporate CEO, ditch-digger, or stay-at-home mom or dad, you spend a lot of your life working. Work is a good thing, but wouldn't it be great to invest your work time in something that brings you happiness and fulfillment? I know circumstances often dictate that we have to do the uncomfortable and unpleasant things because of our adult responsibilities, but if you find yourself in a job you hate, you might consider moving toward a job you love.

If your immediate thought is *I could never do that*, my question to you is *why not?* Who says you can't work toward discovering your desires and skills and then match them to your work? Where is that voice coming from? Whose voice is it? If you listen to the critical voice in your head, you may very well miss all God intends for your life. Identifying what you like and are good at will help you take the first step toward finding fun in your work. Don't play the movie too far forward. Just bloom where you're planted, and take the first step. Every little success seems to build another; soon you'll find your passions and efforts coming together in a life of greater fulfillment and purpose. Consider those who took their "little" talents and desires and moved forward, like Anne Beiler.

Anne Beiler is the founder of the world's largest mall-based pretzel franchise, Auntie Anne's Hand-Rolled Soft Pretzels. Raised in an Amish Mennonite family in Lancaster County, Pennsylvania, Anne viewed the world from the back of a horse-drawn buggy for the first years of her life. As the third of eight children, she grew up with loving parents who taught her many valuable lessons, including showing generosity toward others and having a strong work ethic. While completing her traditional Amish Mennonite schooling, Anne was introduced to the idea of entrepreneurship by baking cakes and pies to sell at area farmers' markets. That business grew from one farmer's market stand in 1988 to a franchise organization with more than nine hundred locations worldwide today. Now Auntie Anne's gives more than a million dollars to charity every year.

If you'd asked Anne Beiler what she was good at and what she enjoyed thirty years ago, she likely would have answered with something like, "Well, I like to bake things and sell them." Who would have imagined that "little" joyful expression of Anne's talents would have grown into such an enterprise? Auntie Anne's Hand-Rolled Soft Pretzels employs thousands of people and affects millions each year with its charity work. You just never know what can happen when you pursue your passion and gifting.

Like it or not, you're going to make the trip of life from cradle to grave—we all do. The question is are you going to enjoy the journey? Is this life just something we endure to get to our final reward, or is it an opportunity to laugh, love, and leave a legacy of joy? What if it's both? In the Christian faith we do believe in a life to come and a hope for an eternal resting place with God. And Scripture is clear that the journey in this earthly life will not always be pleasant. Jesus said, "In this world you will have trouble. But take heart! I have overcome the world" (John 16:33).

Arming yourself with the knowledge that life will inevitably have bad parts will equip you to also recognize and embrace the good parts. Neither the good nor the bad last forever, and your life will be a mix of both. Are you looking for and grasping the good in your life? Or is your focus primarily on the struggles? Sometimes you have to intentionally look for the good. In his book *Anxiety and Depression Boot Camp*, Dr. Marino suggests beginning each day with a simple "gratitude log." Taking a few minutes each day to write down five things you're grateful for will help you frame your life with a more accurate perspective. You'll begin to realize that your life is not all bad, that it is a mix of good *and* bad. Intentionally searching for and finding some good in your life will help you enjoy your journey.

WHAT ABOUT YOUR RELATIONSHIPS?

Are they fun-filled or something less than pleasurable? Of course, many of our relationships are not of our choosing. We're born or marry into families filled with different personalities. We don't often control whom we work with or who attends our church or other social communities. Still, we do have some choices about the level of intimacy we allow in our relationships. An inventory of your current relationships and what they bring into your life is a good idea. Are there people who bring you joy, fun, laughter, and love? Move toward them. What about those on the other side of the relationship fence, the people who exhaust and deplete you? Within the bounds of healthy adult responsibility, it may be time to set some appropriate boundaries.

Having boundaries is an often misunderstood concept. Some view boundaries as a tactic to dig in your heels and stand your ground with ferocious intensity. I believe a healthier view of boundaries is that they are personal property lines that mark what is your responsibility and what is not. The great thing about well-set boundaries is that they tend to take the emotion and conflict out of relationships. Your life no longer becomes a negotiation over what you will and will not allow, because those questions are already settled.

More than just limits, you can think of boundaries as guidelines or fences that keep you on track in reaching a better destination. They keep you from veering too far off a healthy and productive path. You can divide boundaries into two categories: external and internal.

External boundaries allow us to choose our distance from other people and things, and enable us to give or refuse permission for them to be in our personal space. For example:

- I'm not going to attend that function if X is there. It is not safe for me. They trigger my emotions and I feel sad and angry.

- I'm not going to the bar. I drink, get depressed, and say and do things I deeply regret later. I then beat myself up for not having the strength to resist.

- I'm going to make new holiday traditions this year. Doing the same things I've done before makes me sad and keeps me stuck in painful past memories. I'm going to stop chasing my pain.

External boundaries are more tangible in nature than internal boundaries.

Internal boundaries are more about what's going on inside of you, inside your body, mind, and spirit. When put into practice, good internal boundaries protect our thoughts, emotions, and feelings. For example:

- I know that I overeat when I'm stressed. Before I run to food for comfort, I'm going to write down what I'm feeling at that moment. This will help me embrace my struggle and examine what's driving those painful feelings.

- When the boss doesn't say good morning, I feel he doesn't like me and I'm doing a bad job. I'm going to remind myself that I cannot read minds and that his actions likely have more to do with what's going on in him and are probably not even related to me.

- When I look in the mirror I feel fat and ugly. Whose voice am I hearing there? That's how my "perfect" sister made me feel. Her condemning voice no longer deserves this place of honor in my life. I am an adult and I can think for myself.

OTHER BENEFITS OF SETTING HEALTHY BOUNDARIES

- **Building trust:** Setting or respecting a boundary shouldn't equal loss, but rather security.

- **Managing your need for approval:** You are less dependent on others.

- **Becoming vulnerable:** You see others' issues as theirs, but also allow yourself a view from their perspective.

- **Handling intimacy:** It becomes your choice and unforced.

- **Reaching your goals:** Boundaries keep you on track.

- **Improving assertive behavior:** You exercise your adult voice.

- **Accepting personal responsibility:** You own your part. Instead of thinking, *That's my responsibility, but . . .* your thinking stops at *That's my responsibility.*

- **Overcoming the role of victim or martyr:** In life there are genuine victims and martyrs. Embracing that role as your identity is a prescription for sadness and failure in life. Starting today you have adult choices and options.

- **Handling confrontation:** Having a firm boundary takes the power from the struggle. It's no longer a negotiation.

- **Handling forgiveness:** Some can't forgive, while some can't accept forgiveness. Assigning accurate responsibility clears the picture.

- **Decreasing passive aggressiveness:** Poor boundaries foster hostile dependency. You don't speak up; you internalize the pain and take it out on others in subtle ways.

- **Developing self-control:** Defining your limits helps you accept responsibility for your behavior. You don't feel the need to react to the external circumstances, but rather you respond to your internal values.

Take a few moments to jot down the relationships you have in order of how much time you spend with each person. Now rate them as to the amount of joy and good things they bring into your life. After comparing the two lists, you may wish to reconsider where you invest your relationship time.

The cliché is "Life is short, enjoy it." That's one of those clichés that got to be a cliché because it's true. If you're older than forty, you probably realize that life goes by all too quickly. No, you will not enjoy every part of life, but are you havin' any fun at all? I hope so. Let's do a checkup by answering these questions:

- When was the last time you really laughed?
- Is laughter a regular part of your life?
- What do you really enjoy doing? How often do you do it?
- Do you sleep well? If not, what could you do to enhance your sleep?
- What are you really good at? Do you enjoy it? Are you pursuing it? If not, why not?
- Who brings joy into your life? How much time do you spend with them?
- Do you have a "bucket list," that is, things you'd like to do before you pass into eternity? What are those things? What's keeping you from pursuing them?

Chapter 8

TI:
TIME IS
VALUABLE—
USE IT
WISELY

I T'S VERY "TIMELY" (pardon the pun) as I'm writing this chapter that *all* of the Gatlins have been together this week to celebrate my parent's sixty-fifth wedding anniversary. I've had thirty-four people in my house for the last two days. Thank God they're gone—finally!

Actually, I'm sitting here at my desk with a bit of a lump in my throat reliving our time together this week. The last time we were all together was at my parent's sixtieth wedding anniversary celebration. Five long years have gone by since our entire family has been together. Where does the time go?

The fact that two people can stay married for sixty-five years in this day and time is no small accomplishment. What an example my parents have been to me through all these years! Their four children have grown into a family totaling thirty-four people! There are nine grandchildren and nine great-grandchildren (and still counting!). Since we were last together five years ago, we've had four weddings and four great-grandchildren have been born. So much has transpired in that short period of time. Having my parents, now in their eighties, to the littlest newborn all together under one roof for a few hours was nothing short of miraculous. It was truly amazing . . . and I almost didn't live to see it happen. A few years ago, in the throes of major depression, I nearly took my own life. Here's the way it went down . . .

The thought of *dying* didn't scare me, the thought of *living* did. I had sat all day long with the pill bottles in my hands contemplating what I was about to do. I thought, *LaDonna, you cannot do this to yourself or your family.* So I put the lid back on the pills, took a deep breath, and refused to do the unthinkable. Yet the thought of just going to sleep and never waking up again was very appealing to me. I was reminded of a line in one of my brother's songs, "just existing makes dying look easy," and that's exactly how I felt.

I had been clinically depressed for months. I was afraid of everything and felt completely overwhelmed by life. When my husband, Tim, left for work in the mornings I would go back to bed, curl up with our dog, Jackson Brown, and stay in bed until late afternoon. Our master bedroom is the farthest room from my home office, and I would literally close the doors to the office as if I were closing off that part of my life. My office represented a large part of what I was afraid of—my next career move, learning new technology, being an aging speaker in a world of twenty-somethings. When I closed the bedroom door, I felt safe under those covers.

It's difficult to describe the utter isolation I felt. I have a loving, supportive family and was under a psychiatrist's care. Yet the chemistry in my brain was so imbalanced I could not think rationally. I glanced at the clock to mark the time. At 2:15 PM on that November afternoon, I opened the bottle of prescription sleeping pills for the last time. I counted them out on the kitchen counter. There were thirty-one of them; I took every single one. In my last act of desperate surrender, I lay down in the guest bedroom and went to sleep.

The next thing I remember was waking up in a hospital with Tim calling my name. Doctors and nurses were everywhere, along with other members of my precious family and my pastor. In a fog I asked what had happened, but in my heart the reality of what I'd done began to emerge. Somehow I convinced the doctors that I had accidentally taken only five sleeping pills (in my foggy haze I thought I had!). Incredibly, they bought my story, and even though hospital protocol required they keep suicide patients overnight for observation, they let me go home.

On our ride home, Tim began to tell me what happened. He had come home from work around 5:30 PM and found me asleep in the guest bedroom. He didn't think much of it because

I'd been sleeping a lot in those days. But when he couldn't wake me up, he got very concerned and began to investigate. He went into our master bathroom and saw the empty pill bottles on the counter. I can only imagine the sheer panic that must have gripped him. Tim immediately called 911.

How those bottles got from the kitchen to the master bedroom and the fact that there were several of them is still a complete mystery to me. Evidently after taking the first round of pills, in a stupor, I walked into our master bedroom and took more pills. Tim had found a puddle on the floor. I'm sorry to be so graphic, but whatever I vomited may have saved my life. Upon our arrival back home, there must have been a million unanswered questions running through his mind, but my husband and best friend of thirty-four years just held me until we both fell asleep.

The next morning, as we retraced my steps, it became very clear to us that I had taken more than five sleeping pills. I told Tim what little I could remember and he called my psychiatrist. The doctor immediately checked me into a psychiatric hospital for treatment. I have been in hospitals before (to have my babies and for minor surgeries), but I've never been in a psychiatric unit. It's a whole different world. We arrived about noon and met with countless healthcare professionals. We filled out paperwork for what seemed like hours; it was exhausting. And the one question they kept asking me was, "What are you here for?" I reluctantly, almost shamefully had to answer, "Attempted suicide." Their next question was always, "And what do you do for a living?" It seemed almost comical to answer them when I said, "I'm a motivational speaker."

I was finally assigned to a nurse who took my vitals and weighed me. My normal weight is around 130. I weighed 112 pounds. Then the moment of truth arrived. It was time to be taken back to the psychiatric unit. Tears streaming down our cheeks, Tim and I hugged good-bye, and the heavy steel door shut between us. What I remember about that moment is the silence . . . complete, utter silence. I was now officially on the other side.

The caregiver who escorted me down that long hallway gave me a tour of the place as if she were a Realtor showcasing a beautiful new home. I know she was just trying to alleviate my fears, but my heart was in my throat. Frankly, I could not possibly have cared any less about the facilities at that moment. All I knew is that I was about to go into a psychiatric unit and I was scared to death. We walked through one last set of doors, and there I was, in the dayroom, officially *on the unit*. There were women sitting at card tables coloring in coloring books. *How bizarre*, I thought, *grown women coloring in coloring books!* The nurse at the desk immediately took my bag and began inspecting it for contraband. The drawstrings were removed from my sweat pants and the laces were removed from my tennis shoes.

All of my toiletries were put into a box and placed in a locked room; I couldn't even keep my lip balm! I was informed that toiletries were checked out two times a day, once in the morning and once in the evening. I could shave my legs only if a female tech was available to stand just outside the shower curtain. Likewise, I could use a hair dryer only in the presence of a staff member. From performing before thousands to this— it was one of the most humbling experiences of my life. In the back of my mind I knew I'd crossed a line with my overdose and all these precautions were for my own protection, but it was humiliating.

Family visitation began at 7:00 PM and I counted the minutes until those doors opened. At 7:00 PM on the dot, Tim walked in, and it was a sweet reunion! Our hour together went by much too quickly and suddenly we had to say good-bye. Fighting back tears, I went to my room and wrote in my journal about the unbelievable events of this last thirty hours. I took a shower, and with no staff member available to monitor me, I had to go to bed with wet hair and fuzzy legs. Surprisingly, I slept well that night (thank God my roommate didn't snore!).

Life on the unit took on a certain rhythm. There were group

sessions in the mornings and evenings, and it was during these sessions that I really began to learn about these people and hear their stories. I soon discovered that you really don't know what's going on in someone's life by what you see on the surface. Their stories broke my heart. Still, I welcomed every opportunity to get out of there, even for a few moments. Just walking to the dining room for a meal felt like an outing. The only way I could go outside was if I went with the smokers, and I don't smoke! But I jumped at the chance to go with them.

We had music therapy on Saturdays and Mondays, and I marveled at the devoted music therapist, Rebecca, who led our group. She sat us in a circle of chairs and invited us to choose an instrument from a box in the middle. Saxophones, trumpets—no, I'm talking about instruments that a five-year-old would play at day care. During music therapy the drug and alcohol addiction unit joined us. There were guys with biceps the size of hams covered in tattoos playing toy cymbals and tambourines and singing at the top of their lungs! We were a funky little band to say the least, but our music therapist never wavered. She passed around lyric sheets so we could sing while she played the guitar. She was always sincerely complimentary and enthusiastic about our efforts—what a dedicated lady! I could see she was trying to make a connection with us on any level she possibly could.

There was also a keyboard in the music therapy room, and one day Rebecca asked if anyone played. I looked around and finally, sheepishly, raised my hand. She was thrilled! I walked over to this tiny little keyboard and began to play one of the songs she had passed out to the group. You would have thought I was Liberace! I received nothing but total support and encouragement from Rebecca and the group—how healing it felt.

One evening after dinner, my unit roommate (I'll call her Judy, a very lively gal!) decided we should have a talent show. She'd heard me play the piano during music therapy and asked if I'd accompany those who might want to sing. "Sure," I said. "It's not as if I have to be somewhere else!" I took that opportunity to visit with a precious eighteen-year-old named Emily (not her real name). Emily wore only black and definitely had the "Goth" look going on. Turtlenecks, long sleeves, long skirts or pants, and gloves—always gloves. I discovered why at dinner one night when she removed her gloves to eat. I saw the scars on her hands and wrists. Emily was cutting; that is, she was injuring herself on purpose by making scratches or cuts on her body with a sharp object—enough to make it break the skin and bleed.

I so wanted to reach out to this troubled young lady. I knew she had sung in high school productions, so I hatched a plan. Up to this point we'd made only slight eye contact, so

I cautiously approached her and asked if she'd join us in the unit talent show. Surprisingly, she smiled and quietly said, "I'd love to sing . . . do you know 'Somewhere over the Rainbow'?" By this time I had a huge lump in my throat! "Yes," I said, "but I hope you sing it in the key of G because that's the only key I can play it in!"

The night of the show, Emily began singing, "Somewhere over the rainbow, way up high." I swear, it was as if angels descended from heaven. It felt like a holy moment and part of Emily's journey to healing. I was so thankful to be a part of it. After Emily sang, my roommate, Judy, rallied the troops with the country staple "San Antonio Rose." Oh, how I love country music! It was just what we all needed in order to regain our composure.

At that very moment, the telephone rang at the nurses' station. All three of my brothers were on the other end of the line, calling from their dressing room in Branson, Missouri, where they were performing Christmas shows. They asked if they could speak to me. My brothers knew their little sis was gonna be all right when the desk nurse said, "Sorry, guys . . . she's kinda busy right now playing piano for the talent show here on the unit!" I could hear them howling through the speaker phone! They knew right then and there that *little sis* was going to be okay! I've performed on stages all of my life in front of thousands of people, but that little psych unit concert is still my favorite of all time. Our friend Mac Davis once wrote, "Music is the universal language, and love is the key to brotherhood and peace and understanding and living in harmony." I think he got it right.

To think I might have missed all the good things that have happened in my life since my suicide attempt causes me to shudder. I would have never seen some of my grandbabies being born, never held their little hands, and never known their unique facial expressions. Life is short enough—why would anyone want to rush into eternity before they've completed their time on earth? Dr. Marino, who works with many depressed and suicidal people, puts it this way. "No one wants to kill themselves; they just want the pain to stop." That statement describes my situation completely. The pain had become unbearable, and as I viewed life through my depressed mental filter, I could not see a way out. That's how you think when you're depressed—you really cannot see much hope. Interestingly, people looking on from the outside can often see much hope and possibility for your situation; you just can't see it yourself.

In the healthiest seasons of your life, your thoughts are not completely accurate. When you're depressed, feeling as though you're merely existing and not living, your thoughts are unreliable. No one has the ability to be completely objective about themselves. I thank God for those who cared enough to invest in my life and help me challenge my sad, depressed thoughts. Perhaps the most profound healing came from those who simply walked with me and didn't try to fix me. My husband, my hero Tim, did not lecture me when we left the emergency room. He did not say things like, "It's silly to feel that way," or "Pull yourself up by the bootstraps, LaDonna." He lay down with me in bed and held me. *Presence* always trumps *presents* when it comes to helping someone who's hurting.

Before we move on, I do feel it's important to say a few more words about suicide. As I shared earlier in the book, it's far more common than most realize. According to the National Institute of Health, we average about thirty thousand suicides every year in America. And for every successful suicide, there are at least eight failed attempts like mine. I say *at least* because many failed suicide attempts are never reported.

If you're reading this and feeling like I was, that the pain of your life is just too much to bear, please hear these words: Even though it may feel like it, every day won't be like today. Depression cycles down and up, and your life will be better sooner than later. What you're considering is a permanent solution to a temporary problem. If you can do nothing else, please do this: pick up the phone and dial 1-800-SUICIDE. You have nothing to lose and everything to gain. I'm so glad I didn't miss what God had in store for me beyond my depression. God has something for you too.

Hopefully, you are not suicidal as you read this. You may, however, feel stuck in life and unsure of how to best redeem the time you have left on earth. Understandably, we don't like to think much about it, but the clock is ticking. Our earthly lives are finite. At some point most of us come to grips with our mortality, and that doesn't have to be a somber thought. In a sense, it's healthy to dip our life plans into the pool of reality. We get only so much time to live, love, learn, and experience this life. What are you going to do with the time you have left? Let's consider some options.

- Worry

- Be angry

- Seek fame and fortune

- Prove your worth

- Compete

- Collect lots of stuff

- Hurry

OR

- Love

- Build healthy relationships

- Learn

- Give to others and yourself

- Laugh

- Discover your purpose and passions

- Relax

- Trust God

The truth is, we often hold on tightest to the things that matter the least. If you knew that tomorrow was your last day on earth, how would you spend today? What hidden resentment or lingering bitterness would you release? Whether it's ninety-five years from now or ninety-five minutes from now, your time is coming—mine too. I sometimes find I worry the most about things that matter the least, so perhaps you can relate.

It's natural to hold on to anger, resentment, and bitterness when you've been legitimately wounded by others. One of my favorite quotes is from author Dale Carnegie who said, "Wouldn't our enemies rub their hands with glee if they knew that our hate for them was exhausting us, making us tired and nervous, ruining our looks, giving us heart trouble and probably shortening our lives?" The Old Testament book of Job 5:2 says, "To worry yourself to death with resentment would be a foolish, senseless thing to do (GNT)." It's time to stop letting others control your thoughts, health, and actions. They don't deserve this place of honor in your life.

It seems that spending what's left of our lives thinking about past wrongs is a poor use of our time. Forgiveness, in the Christian faith context, is really about releasing justice to God. Are you ready to let it go? Of course, releasing justice does not mean you allow unsafe and toxic people a place in your life. Proper adult boundaries mandate that we protect ourselves and our loved ones. But focusing your life on some past hurt or injury is not how you'll finish the race well. You will not look back at the end of the trail and think, *I wish I had more time to be ticked off at them.* It's more likely that you'll regret that you ever gave them a second thought.

What are you going to do with the great gift you have of the rest of your life? This is where the automatic negative thoughts might begin to creep in. *I can't do* (fill in the blank.) *I'm too old. I don't have the money. I'm not smart enough*, and so on. As we addressed in Chapter 6, to a certain extent we all have to play with the cards we're dealt. Before you consider what you *can't* do with the time you have left, consider what you *can* do. A few years can go a long way. Consider the brief life of Mattie Stepanek.

Matthew Joseph Thaddeus Stepanek won worldwide acclaim as a poet, a spokesperson for the physically challenged, and a peace advocate—all before he passed away at age thirteen in 2004. Mattie had six books of poetry and one book of essays that were all on the *New York Times* best sellers list. He stirred crowds with powerful oratory and even lobbied on Capitol Hill on behalf of people with disabilities and children with life-threatening conditions.

Mattie suffered from a rare form of muscular dystrophy. His sister and two brothers died from the disease during early childhood and his mother has the adult form, which was diagnosed after all four of her children were born.

At the age of three, little Mattie started to write poetry to cope with the death of his older brother. In 2002, he began a three-term appointment as the Muscular Dystrophy Association's National Goodwill Ambassador. In 2003, country music star Billy Gilman, who became friends with Mattie, released an album called *Music Through Heartsongs: Songs Based on the Poems of Mattie J. T. Stepanek*. The album reached number fifteen on the U.S. Top Country chart, and Mattie can be heard reciting his poetry on several tracks.

Let's recap: All three of Mattie's siblings died at an early age, his mom also has muscular dystrophy, and Mattie himself was confined to a wheelchair for most of his short life. He passed into eternity one month short of his fourteenth birthday. I'm certain one of the great temptations of Mattie's life was to think of the many legitimate reasons he could not do things. Rather, he focused his energies on what he *could* do. What about you?

Here's another example. A few years back at one of the large, arena-style Christian women's conferences, Joni Eareckson Tada was scheduled to be the opening speaker. You may know of Joni. Her life has been chronicled in a movie and best-selling autobiography entitled *Joni*. As a teenager she was enjoying a summer vacation before preparing to go to college in the fall. She dove into what she thought was a safe section of Chesapeake Bay, only to discover it was far too shallow. She broke her neck and has been a quadriplegic, unable to move from the neck down, ever since.

That hard reality has led her on a lifelong search for God's truth and answers to help people who, like her, have to deal with harsh, seemingly unexplainable tragedy. She has become a prolific author, in-demand speaker, media personality, and tireless advocate for disability rights. Since becoming paralyzed in 1967, Joni has faced difficulty every single day beyond what most will ever know.

At that recent women's conference there was a poignant moment that underscored how our perspective shapes what we do with the rest of our lives. For some reason the seating plan for the floor in the arena was fouled up. Some women had tickets with the same seat numbers on them and others had tickets for seats that didn't exist. As the confusion built, the noise and complaining level began to rise. The women became so upset that the rumble from the arena could be heard backstage in the speaker's area. Without an introduction, Joni asked to be wheeled onto the stage while the frantic light and sound crew scrambled to turn on her microphone and lights. The somewhat baffled crowd began to settle as Joni lovingly stared at them from her wheelchair at center stage. As the thousands of women quieted, Joni cleared her throat and said, "I understand some of you are not happy with your seat." Wow—in that very sentence she gave them an incredible gift of perspective. The crowd roared with approval at the simple lesson Joni had modeled. You can embrace what you have or wallow in the quick-drying cement of what you do not. You have a choice.

Perhaps the greatest story from Scripture concerning embracing what you have comes from 1 Samuel chapter 17. Most are somewhat familiar with the story of David and Goliath, but if you need a bit of a refresher, here's a brief summary: The Philistine army had gathered for war against Israel. The two armies camped on opposite sides of a steep valley. A Philistine giant measuring more than nine feet tall and wearing full armor came out every day for forty days, mocking and challenging the Israelites to fight. His name was Goliath. Even the Israelite king Saul, who was the tallest in his army, was terrified of Goliath.

One day a young teenager named David, the youngest son of Jesse, was sent to the battle lines by his father to bring back news about his brothers. Upon approaching the front battle lines, David heard Goliath shouting his daily defiance and he saw how much it scared the men in the army of Israel. David shouted to the frightened troops, "Who is this Philistine that he should defy the armies of God?"

So David volunteered to fight Goliath. While it took some persuasion, King Saul finally agreed to let David fight the giant. Dressed in just his simple tunic, carrying his slingshot and a pouch full of stones, David approached Goliath. The giant cursed at him, yelling threats and insults.

David said to Goliath, "You come against me with sword and spear and javelin, but I come against you in the name of the LORD Almighty, the God of the armies of Israel, whom you have defied . . . today I will give the carcasses of the Philistine army to the birds of the air . . . and the whole world will know that there is a God in Israel . . . it is not by sword or spear that the LORD saves; for the battle is the LORD's, and he will give all of you into our hands (vv. 45–47)".

As Goliath moved in for the kill, David reached into his bag and slung one of his stones at Goliath's head. The stone sank deep into the giant's forehead and he fell facedown on the ground. David then took Goliath's sword, killed him, and then cut off his head. When the Philistines saw that their hero was dead, they turned and ran. The army of the Israelites pursued, chasing and killing them, and the victory was theirs.

There is great "takeaway value" from this story for you. David used what he had and did not focus on what he did not. He did not protect himself with armor, as anyone of that day marching into a life-and-death struggle would. David was unfamiliar with the feel of armor and stayed within what he was comfortable with—his simple slingshot, a weapon he was skilled at using. Very often God will use the unique skills he has already placed in your hands. Just be yourself and use the familiar gifts and talents God has given you. He can work miracles through you.

Another point to consider is that David's faith in God caused him to look at the giant from a different perspective. He saw Goliath as a mortal man defying an all-powerful God. David looked at the battle from God's point of view. If we look at giant problems and impossible situations from God's perspective, we realize that God will fight with us. What seems impossible in our own strength becomes possible in God's strength.

David was clear in his mind about his purpose. He did not allow criticism and doubt to creep into his spirit. When the giant insulted and threatened, David didn't stop or even waver. Only God's opinion mattered to David, he did not allow fear to be his rudder. David steered a clear and steadfast course.

Perhaps you're facing a giant problem or impossible situation today. Rest for a moment, reflect on your mission, and refocus. Can you see the situation more clearly from God's vantage point? Your perspective is essential in applying your energy and efforts. Do not be confused; courage is not the absence of fear. Courage is doing the right thing in the face of your fears. Remember, God's opinion is the only one that really matters.

Often in the midst of struggle you can see only the "giants" or pile of problems before you. It's natural to be overwhelmed when you view your future from the valley and gaze only at the distant mountaintop. Rather than focus your eyes and energies on the end result of your efforts, it's helpful to just take one step at a time. Do what's in front of you, use the tools you *do* have, and don't try to predict the outcome. With every small step toward your goal, you'll begin to see your future unfold. You will gain strength as you exercise your physical and spiritual muscles. You will find wisdom in the lessons learned on the journey and soon discover that, in God's economy, nothing is wasted—no hurt, no struggle, and no amount of pain. At the end of your life's journey, you will find that moving forward and just doing what you're able to do was, in fact, the very best use of your time on earth.

As we discussed earlier, your time is finite. In the scope of eternity, your view back on this life will be measured, in large part, by how you redeemed the time you were given. Of course, your views on eternity are colored by what you believe—that's something you'll have to explore and determine for yourself. In the Christian faith we believe there is a better, eternal life to come, as we embrace God's grace and forgiveness through the sacrifice of Christ. But we're still here for now, so what's your purpose for the time you have left? What are you going to do with what you have? Consider these questions:

- Why I am I here? Do I have a purpose?

- How much time do I spend thinking about things I cannot change?

- What would I really like to do to apply what I have?

- What's stopping me from making the most of my time?

- Where could I step out in faith and stretch myself a bit?

- What unimportant thing am I holding on to that I could let go of?

Chapter 9

THAT
WILL BRING
US BACK TO
DO!

I NTERESTINGLY ENOUGH, we finish our little musical adventure right where we began, by doing the right thing. Making the decision more than thirty years ago to leave the Gatlin family group, follow my heart, and sing a different song has taken me on an incredible journey. I've sung my song on the stage of the Grand Ole Opry in Nashville. I've sung my song at the Crystal Cathedral in California. I've sung my song in the form of lullabies to my own newborn babies and grand-babies, and I've even sung my song in the prison cells of death row. I've found one thing to be true in all of those places—a song can be a powerful thing.

I'll never forget the day a young female prison inmate came up to me and said, "LaDonna, I can remember living only two places in my entire lifetime—under a bridge in Dallas and behind these prison walls." I was speechless, and that seldom happens! So I stood there for what felt like an eternity and finally, with tears streaming down our cheeks, I did the only thing I knew to do. I sang this song:

> *Amazing grace,*
> *How sweet the sound*
> *That saved a wretch like me.*
> *I once was lost, but now am found*
> *Was blind but now I see*

The song . . . the power of song has taken me on an incredible journey. It's brought me here to you today to tell you that *you* have your own song to sing. Whether you're an opera star or can't carry a tune in a bucket, you are, in a sense, singing the notes of your life every day. Through your words and deeds, you're shaping your life and the lives of countless others. I want to encourage you with all my heart to find your song and sing it loud and clear. You just never know who might need to hear it. It might be me.

Or it might be my daughter, as it was on that November morning in 1999 when I received a phone call from the school nurse at her high school. (May I just pause here to say thank God for school nurses who know when to make tough phone calls to parents!)

Annie had driven off to school like she had every other morning of her senior year. It seemed like just another day in the life of a high school senior, but that changed dramatically when I answered the phone. The nurse said, "LaDonna, I have

Annie here in my office with me. She needs to talk to you." Annie got on the phone. I could barely understand her through her tears, but there was no mistaking these three words when she said, "Mom, I'm pregnant."

Talk about shock. I realize that we are not the first family to whom this has happened, nor will we be the last. But it was the first time it had ever happened to our family. I asked Annie if she could come home, and the nurse said, "Sure, honey, go home." While Annie was en route, I called Tim, who was on his way to work. He made a giant U-turn and hurried back to the house. Tim and Annie arrived at the same time; he came in the back door just as she came in the front, and we just held one another and cried for a long while.

Finally, we gained some level of composure and sat down in the living room to discuss where to go from here. I called the school, and as I began explaining the situation to the sweet lady who answered the phone, she stopped me and transferred me to the guidance counselor. At first I wasn't quite sure where this whole conversation was heading, but it soon became clear that this wasn't his first time dealing with this. He gently embraced our situation with open arms. He began to list all the things he was going to do for our daughter to make sure she completed her studies so she could graduate with her class. He even went so far as to share a very personal story about his own sister who'd been through this very same situation. "I've been down this road, both personally and professionally, and here's what we're going to do," he said. There was not one inkling of disapproval or judgment from this man. He simply sang his song to us, and it sounded like a beautiful symphony because, at that moment, we really weren't sure we could face the music!

Skip forward five months. Annie walked across the stage in May 2000 (very obviously seven months pregnant!) and received her diploma with her graduating class. A few days later, she got a handwritten note from her school superintendent. It began, "Annie, I'm so proud of you! You've completed your high school education on time and have been a role model for other young women who might find themselves in a similar situation." Wow!

Two months later Annie gave birth to a healthy eight-and-a-half-pound baby boy. His name is Hayden and he *is* the "Bugerhead" you read about in Chapter 3! But the story gets even better! Annie is now a special education teacher in that same school district. She's married to a teacher-coach and has a beautiful family—all because a group of educators sang *their* song to our daughter. It made a huge difference in her world, and we can only imagine the good things to come. You truly never know the impact you can have when you step out to sing your song and do the right thing.

This chapter, and this book for that matter, talks a lot about doing the right thing. Many times the choice is ours, and our actions can have great power. Moving forward with proactive intention is often a key to finding meaning, purpose, and hope in life—and shaping the lives of others.

However, sometimes our actions are more *reactions* than actions, because life can throw us curveballs. As we discussed earlier, we have limited control in life. Attempting to control the outcome of everything tends to lead to frustration, sadness, anxiety, and depression. Sometimes doing the right thing is little more than controlling our reactions to great challenges.

Such was the case for Tim and me some thirty years ago. Tim is a two-time cancer survivor. His first bout was in 1982, when our son was just three years old and our daughter was a newborn. My memories of those days are mixed. On one hand I was terrified of being a young mother and facing the loss of my husband. On the other, I had an odd peace and swelling of pride for Tim's uncommonly mature and godly strength.

Tim had gone into the hospital for what we thought was exploratory surgery, but the doctor walked into the waiting room with a look of grave concern on his face that shook me to my core. He said, "LaDonna, I have some good news and I have some bad news. The good news is, we think we got it all." That was the good news? Got what? He went on to say that my husband had testicular cancer and that Tim would need to undergo radiation treatments to make sure they got it all. He was only twenty-seven years old.

With hopeful expectation we embarked on the journey to the MD Anderson Cancer Hospital in Houston to begin six weeks of unpleasant radiation treatment. I was still breast-feeding our newborn daughter at the time, which made things more difficult to say the least. By God's grace and with the prayers and practical help from our amazing family and friends, we made it through. Tim was pronounced cancer free a few months later—hallelujah!

Fast-forward to June 2009. I was sitting in the Pittsburg airport waiting for a flight when my cell phone rang. It was Tim. His worst fears had been realized when he got the PSA report back from his urologist: prostate cancer. *Please, God,* I thought, *not again!* But indeed, we were in for another battle with cancer. This time Tim had surgery and, thankfully, today my best friend and husband of thirty-seven years is alive and well. Now, I tell you this story with the full knowledge that sometimes the cancer story doesn't turn out so well. Undoubt-edly, you've known people who've battled cancer and did not survive.

Does that mean God likes Tim and me better or that he was not faithful because others' prayers for healing weren't answered? I don't think so. Sometimes doing the right thing is little more than doing what you *can* do and trusting God for the outcome. I believe Tim's reaction and his dignified response to difficulty had its roots in his faith. Faced with losing his own life, he remained my rock. I'm sure he was afraid, as any normal person would be, when confronting his mortality. Yet Tim did not allow his fear to prevent him from moving forward and doing the right—albeit difficult—things. I return to the premise of Chapter 6: *What are you going to do with what you have?* Consider the story of young Jessica Joy Rees.

From the outside looking in, Jessie was not unlike many other grade school kids growing up in Orange County, California. She was part of a model family. Her older sister Shaya, her younger brother J.T., her mom, Stacey, and her dad, Erik, were the picture of what most would see as a happy household. Erik was a longtime pastor at Rick Warren's Saddleback Church, and their lives were strongly intertwined with a healthy community and a commitment to serving others.

Little did they imagine how their lives would change over the span of just a few short months. On March 3, 2011, just weeks short of her twelfth birthday, Jessica was diagnosed with a brain stem tumor. Her doctors offered little hope for the family, and their tragedy was compounded just a few months later when a second tumor was discovered.

After an exhaustive nationwide search for the best pediatric cancer treatment hospitals, they determined Children's Hospital of Orange County, near their home, was the place to be. So, armed with their faith and the prayers of their church family, they began an arduous radiation treatment regime. Two weeks into their daily journeys back and forth to the hospital, Jessie paused on the way home to ask her dad a question. "Dad, we get to go home after my treatments. Where do all the other kids getting treatments at the hospital go?" Her dad told her they had to live in the hospital. Without hesitation Jessie responded, "Can we do something for them? Cancer makes you lonely!"

After a bit of research the Rees family learned that in America alone, approximately fifty thousand kids are "guests" in pediatric cancer wards every night. Jessie was determined to do something for them. She decided that, while she couldn't cure their disease, she still had the capacity to care. Jessie began to pack little brown sacks with toys, stickers, and personal notes of encouragement to bring to the cancer ward kids. Soon, the family determined that plastic jars were a more suitable container and, taking a cue from Jessie's middle name, they started packing "JoyJars" to give away. "I still can't get my arms around what she did," says her dad, Erik. What started as a little girl's desire to help care for her fellow sufferers has now blossomed into a worldwide movement. Jessie's dream was to put a JoyJar into the hands of every kid in every cancer unit in every hospital in the world.

Jessie passed into eternity on January 5, 2012, and did not live to see her dream completed—or did she? Like all of us, the legacy we leave behind, doing what we can with what we have, continues to impact others long after we're gone. As of this writing, more than 150,000 people have carried on Jessie's dream, and that number grows every day. Thousands of JoyJars have made their way into the hands of lonely cancer-stricken kids in nearly fifty different countries; 115 children's hospitals in the United States have also adopted the program as well as 175 Ronald McDonald Houses. More than 4,500 people packed Jessie's memorial service while another 4,000 watched live online. At that service more than 300 people decided to turn their hearts toward God and embrace salvation, hope, and help through Jesus Christ. Not bad for a twelve-year-old girl with terminal cancer. How easy and understandable it would have been for the Rees family to turn inward and isolate in their pain. Jessie and the family decided to do the right thing in the face of impossible odds—they took what they had and did what they could. Was it worth it? You'd have to ask the frightened kid sitting in a hospital far from home who is facing pain and an uncertain future who gets an encouraging JoyJar. I think you know the answer. (If you'd like to know more about the ongoing work of the Jessie Rees Foundation, or maybe even get involved yourself, you can connect with them online at www.Jessie.org.)

Of course, knowing the right thing to do and doing it are two different things. Many times we know what actions would be helpful but find ourselves simply unable to move. That's far more common than you might think, the dilemma of feeling stuck mentally, emotionally, physically, and spiritually. Dr. Marino will tell you that one of the most common complaints his counseling clients express is the feeling of being "stuck" in their life circumstances and not being able to move past their pain. He hears the phrase, "I just don't know what to do," on a regular basis. What *do* you do when you just don't know what to do?

First, take a look at your life as a "line" or continuum. There is a start and a finish. A straight, even line would represent life lived on an even keel, steady and consistent, without major ups or downs. Of course, in reality no one has ever lived a life like that. Everyone's life consists of ups and downs. The ups and downs vary in intensity and frequency from person to person and life season to life season, but in some fashion we're all coming out of an up or down cycle—or heading into one.

For most, the ups and downs aren't too deep and don't last too long, but at some point we're all likely to face a deep valley—perhaps the loss of a loved one, a divorce, or the failure of a dream. In the midst of a valley in a down cycle, it is difficult, sometimes impossible, to see anything other than the giant hill that lies before you. You cannot envision a time or circumstance where your life will look different. You literally do not possess the ability to be objective.

Others, looking from the outside, can likely see possibilities and hope for you. From the inside, you see only the hill. You find yourself wrestling with the distorted thinking patterns that are part of life's painful experiences. Predominantly, your mind is trapped in the "all or nothing" thinking that screams that things are all good or all bad, with nothing in between. In reality, everyone and everything (at least in this world) has good parts and bad parts. But from the very bottom of your season of pain, it all looks bad, at least from your view.

Interestingly, during your toughest moments you can likely see hope and good possibilities for others, just not for yourself. This, in itself, breeds a hostile resentment, as you see others' lives working out and yours continuing to spiral downward. This confirms your feelings of hopelessness. There's the sense that there are two sets of rules in the world: one for everyone else that has possibility and one for you that is hopeless. Granted, that sounds a little absurd to say out loud, but when you're deep in the pit of a struggle, you really can come to believe that everyone and everything is against you. You take the world's and God's perceived assault on you personally and can't understand why the deck is so stacked. Are you that bad and deserving of pain? Perhaps that thought reinforces what you've been taught and come to believe about yourself. Deep struggle seems to challenge our self-worth on every level.

Since we've talked quite a bit about our thoughts, feelings, and actions in this book, let's examine them in light of this question: What are the thoughts, feelings, and actions associated with feeling stuck and not knowing what to do?

Thoughts

- I don't know what to do.

- This is never going to get better.

- I want the pain to stop—I'd rather be dead.

- No one understands or cares.

- Even if they did care, no one can help me. It's a lost cause.

- God doesn't exist, doesn't care, or is mad at me.

- I don't matter to anyone or anything. My existence is meaningless. No one is on my side or rooting for me.

Feelings

- Fear

- Sadness

- Shame (I should be able to handle this.)

- Hopelessness

- Tired (I'm worn out and exhausted.)

- Tense (I'm always on edge.)

- Worried (If I worry enough it will change things.)

- Angry (It shouldn't be like this. It's unfair.)

- Unconnected and lonely

- Abandoned and betrayed

- Burdened (I'm carrying too much to bear.)

Actions

- Isolation (I'm going to figure this out myself.)

- Self-medication (drugs, alcohol, tobacco, food, sex, porn)

- Conflict-seeking behavior (bad connection often feels better than no connection)

- Self-harm (cutting, suicide, not taking your meds)

- Spending or hoarding (as if you're going to buy or save your way out of this; it's something you can control in an out-of-control world)

- Impulsive behavior (quick marriage, divorce, an affair, trips with no plans, quitting your job, ending friendships)

So, when you can't think of a reason to get out of bed, go to work, or even keep on living, how *can* you bring yourself to make helpful decisions and do the right thing with what you have?

First, break it down to the smallest thing you can do and concentrate on that only. Perhaps it's brushing your teeth, shaving, or taking a shower. It may take you hours to do just one of those things. Set one very small goal and just focus on that—don't look down the road. When you complete it, you'll feel a sense of accomplishment. Don't make a long list in your head, it will overwhelm you. One small thing at a time; just do what's in front of you.

Second, wrestle with your thoughts in two ways. First, remind yourself that your current thoughts, feelings, and actions are normal for someone who is struggling. Give yourself a break. It's understandable and to be expected. *Second*, remember, every day won't be like this. The ups and downs of your life will cycle and sooner or later, you won't feel this bad. Even though the pain feels unending right now, it is not. This is temporary. You can make it through—millions have.

Next, make attempts to connect with someone. I say *attempts* because you may have to try several times. The phone is good, but in-person is much better. In-person forces you to move— either to get out of the house or at least off the couch to answer the door. In Alcoholics Anonymous the people who have the highest success rate, by far, are those who have a good relationship with their sponsors. During your higher functioning times begin to put together an "emergency" contact list. Tell these people you may be calling them if you get in trouble and let them know they can do the same with you. If you don't have the basis for a relationship list like this, make "connection" opportunities like support groups or community projects a priority during your "good" times.

It's important to have as many people as you can on your list for two reasons. One, the more you have, the more likely you'll be to find someone available when you need them. Two, no one person could or should be the repository for all your problems. They will wear out, just as you would if the roles were reversed. This is what kills many marriages. No one person can be your dumping ground, but everyone needs places to dump.

The next step is to move. Any way, any how. Walk, swim, ride a bike, march in place, stretch, and if at all possible, do it with a friend. Nothing bad can come from this. It has significant mood-altering brain chemistry implications, and it will reinforce accurate thinking. Again, with movement comes a sense of accomplishment and possibility instead of failure and hopelessness.

Finally, it will help you to pray. Of course, we're all coming from different places on the faith spectrum, and the thought of praying may feel very cliché and useless to your struggling mind. Again, break it down to the shortest prayer you can muster. Ask God for help. *Help!* Be honest. If you don't believe your prayer is being heard, be honest about that. But Scripture has an interesting take on hopeless prayers. Matthew 7:7–8 says, "Ask and it will be given to you; seek and you will find; knock and the door will be opened to you. For everyone who asks receives; he who seeks finds; and to him who knocks, the door will be opened."

Now you may be thinking, *Yeah, right . . . tried that, didn't work—still struggling.* It's almost as if God knew you'd be thinking that, so here's the next line of that scripture: "Which of you, if your son asks for bread, will give him a stone? Or if he asks for a fish, will give him a snake? If you, then, though you are evil, know how to give good gifts to your children, how much more will your Father in heaven give good gifts to those who ask him" (vv. 9–11).

Okay, that gives you something to think about. If God is real and God is good, wouldn't he at least help me as much as I'd help one of my kids? Do my kids always see it when I help them or feel they're being helped when I allow pain into their lives? Still, the understandable thought may persist, *If God sees how bad I'm hurting, why doesn't he just step in and fix it? I would not let my kids suffer like this*!

That's a legitimate thought and question. Why is there suffering? I'm not sure, but I *am* sure there are some good things that come only from suffering—things like courage, character, wisdom, maturity, perseverance, and empathy for other sufferers. In addition to all the rotten stuff, your suffering gives you a unique perspective and capacity to know what pain feels like. So with that in mind, God closes this section of Scripture with an action step. It's the Golden Rule: "So in everything, do to others what you would have them do to you" (v. 12). In other words, treat other people like you would want them to treat you. That will show them how you'd like to be treated, and it will get you out of yourself and into someone else. It takes the focus off your pain and helps to create an environment where you can build meaningful relationships that *are* healing and helpful.

I would add that during the dark times, it is equally important to know what *not* to do. These are some of the very destructive habits you can easily fall into as you spiral down into an emotional valley:

Don't bury your head in the computer. You can surf endlessly, engage in fantasy of all kinds, and settle for a false "cyberlife." Yes, sending e-mails, even chatting, is a way of connecting and not necessarily a bad thing. But your computer can become toxic medication and escape. Additionally, it keeps you isolated from actual human contact and reinforces sedentary behavior, which is harmful for your brain function.

Similarly, don't bury your head in the TV. Such choices we have today! Hundreds of channels. Endless channel switching can be very harmful when you're seeking to get unstuck and move through your painful season. TV isn't evil, but it can serve as an unnatural and unfruitful stimulant that only leaves you wanting more. It, like the computer, is most often used in isolation and while sedentary. The TV can have a hypnotic effect that will keep you riveted in destructive solitude for hours. Isolation is the enemy of movement toward hope.

During the tough times, don't make big decisions. Usually, decisions made in the valley of a down cycle have two bad outcomes: (1) they are impulsive and short-sighted, or (2) they are too grandiose for reality. For example, buying a gun and killing yourself. That's a permanent solution for a temporary problem, as we discussed earlier in the book, but people do it all the time. It's an impulsive decision made to stop the pain. Other impulsive and short-sighted actions, like buying a Ferrari, a new house, or lots of new expensive clothing, are all just ill-fated attempts to medicate your pain. They won't work.

Or you may set yourself up to fail with grandiose plans to "turn your life around." You spend a lot of time and energy formulating big plans—a strict exercise regime, new diet, new job, more schooling, getting married, more discipline in your spiritual life, and so on. With every good intention, the list becomes an overwhelming monster and creates more evidence of your inability to do anything. You paralyze yourself by making the task too big.

Look at it like joining a gym. If you're in great shape, running every day, or doing aerobics at home, you won't have much trouble transitioning to the slightly different exercise routines. But if you're out of shape and you join a gym and run really fast until you're completely exhausted on the first visit, you'll be so sore you likely won't come back. It's just too hard. Moreover, it wasn't a good experience. If you're in the pit of a painful reality and try to sprint to the mountaintop, you're setting yourself up for failure. Don't do that—set yourself up to succeed by eating the whale in little bites.

Another trap is setting timetables. Again, this sets you up to fail, so don't do this to yourself. Rather than thinking, *I'm going to do X by a certain time,* leave it at, *I'm going to do X.* Then take on the biggest part of X you can manage and move forward. As long as you're moving forward, you are winning. You are in the recovery process.

During the dark times, do not trust your judgment. Enlist as much helpful counsel as you can. Look for the safe, sane voices that can speak truth into your life. The healthiest of people can rarely be objective about themselves. In the pit of your deep pain, you are not objective. Get some outside eyes on your situation to assist you in decision making and planning.

Let's recap our key points and keep them in mind as you continue your journey to doing the right things, the helpful things that will ultimately take you and those around you to a better place.

Do This . . .

- Break it down to the smallest thing you can do and concentrate on that only.

- Give yourself a break. What's happening to you is understandable. It doesn't make you bad.

- Remind yourself that this is temporary.

- Connect with as many safe, sane people as possible. Don't isolate.

- Move.

- Pray.

Don't Do This . . .

- Bury your head in the computer.

- Bury your head in the TV.

- Make big decisions.

- Set timetables.

- Trust your judgment.

Let's close this chapter with a look at what doing the right thing for you means. If you're ever going to find the song in you, it's so very important to intentionally look for it. What do you like? What are you good at? What gets you excited in life? Many women and men across America have told me they've never given themselves permission to even ask these questions.

Somehow we get so locked in to others' expectations or our own internal pressure to be "something" that we never consider that God may actually have designed us in a certain way for a certain purpose!

Think of it like the oxygen masks on a plane. You know the drill, "Put your own mask on first before you assist anyone else." Isn't that a selfish thing to do? Of course not! We can't help anyone if we run out of oxygen. Sometimes that inaccurate, "selfish" thought creeps into our thinking when we try to figure out who we really are and try to discover our personal vision, values, and voice.

It's not selfish. If you don't do the right thing for yourself, you'll be of little value to others. Put on your oxygen mask first if you want to be the best parent, spouse, sibling, or friend you can be. It's okay to care for yourself; it does not make you bad, as so many of us have come to believe. Being your best self will equip you for a life filled with purpose, meaning, service, and genuine influence for good in others' lives. Take a few moments to consider these questions:

- What is my *song*?

- Whom should I be singing it to?

- What is keeping me from singing loud and clear?

- When have I missed my chance to do the right thing?

- What one right thing can I do today?

- Who has invested in my life by singing their song?

Chapter 10

I Sing Because I'm Happy

A S WE CLOSE OUR TIME TOGETHER, I'd like to take a moment to return to the music. I've used musical metaphors throughout the book because music really does seem to be a universal connecting point. We all have a visceral reaction to music. An upbeat song tends to give us a burst of energy. You've probably seen that person at the stoplight in the car next to you rocking away, singing their lungs out, and playing air drums—or perhaps you've *been* that person!

You've likely noticed that when athletes prepare for the "big game," they're either wearing earbuds or there is music playing in the locker room to get them "psyched." Even doctors sometimes listen to their favorite tunes in the operating room to enhance their concentration.

Remember the national hysteria when Elvis came onto the scene or when the Beatles came to America? When the Beatles made their American TV debut on *The Ed Sullivan Show* in 1964, 73 million people watched. That show is still one of the highest-rated programs in broadcasting history. During the performance you couldn't get a taxi in New York City, and even the crime rate went down. The amazing power of music!

Just last night I watched a replay of Billy Joel's "Last Play at Shea" concert at Shea Stadium, and I got goose bumps, especially when Paul McCartney surprised the crowd by walking onstage and singing with the "Piano Man." I wondered what must have been going through Paul McCartney's mind; surely he was reminiscing about the Beatles' sold-out concert at that very same stadium in 1965. While the music has changed through the years, the crowd was no less moved and enthusiastic.

Most of us have musical memories or certain songs that instantly evoke vivid memories and transport us to another time, place, or life experience. My son and I have a crazy musical Christmas tradition. I'm a Karen Carpenter fan. I know I'm giving away my age here (remember the Carpenters in the 1970s?). She was an alto singer, like me, and most of her songs were in my range. Each Christmas whoever hears her song "Merry Christmas, Darling" first immediately calls the other one. It's a fun tradition. Once I was shopping at the Gap when I heard it. I started crying right then and there. The sales associate, who was about sixteen, said, "Ma'am, are you okay?" I said, "Yes, I'm just having a moment with Karen Carpenter." She sheepishly asked, "Who is Karen Carpenter?" I worked through my emotions of feeling old and quickly called my son, Caleb, to share our musical Christmas connection.

I've observed that even the most unmusical people still love music. Everyone seems to have a favorite style or artist that really speaks to them. I look at it kind of like ice cream; some like vanilla, some like chocolate, and some are tutti-frutti fans—it's very subjective! From emotional, biological, psychological, and spiritual perspectives, music has great power. Think about it; almost every church service starts with or includes music. Massage therapists usually play soothing music in the background, and sporting event crowds are energized when the band plays their team's "fight song." There's a reason why music has such great power in our lives—it's the way we're designed.

Did you know that music is mentioned more than 120 times in the Bible? Did you know that God sings? That's what the Old Testament prophet Zephaniah proclaimed: "The LORD your God is with you, the Mighty Warrior who saves. He will take great delight in you; in his love he will no longer rebuke you, but will rejoice over you with singing" (3:17). God sings? Can you imagine what that sounds like? I guess we'll find out soon enough, but it's clear that music has been hardwired into our brains and souls.

Any mom knows that even babies in the womb react to music. Music really is in our genes. Brain science researchers tell us that music can enhance our brain function, memory, and emotions in a very powerful way. For example, hearing "our romantic song" at a wedding anniversary can bring tears of joy and loving connection, while hearing the same song after a divorce can trigger tears of intense sadness and loss. Music moves our emotions.

It can also make you smarter. Learning to play a musical instrument has also been shown to enhance brain function. In a study by researchers at the University of California, Irvine, thirty-four preschoolers were given piano keyboard training. After six months, all the children could play basic melodies from Mozart and Beethoven. They exhibited significant increases in visual spatial skill (up to a 36 percent improvement) compared to other preschoolers who received computer lessons or other types of stimulation. The College Entrance Examination Board reported in 1996 that students with experience in musical performance scored fifty-one points higher on the verbal part of the SAT and thirty-nine points higher on the math section than the national average.

Music literally moves us. When music engages our brains, we begin to tap our feet, dance, or sing along. Music is almost always coupled with action; it's hard to sit still when the right music begins to percolate in our hearts and souls. It's inspiring to listen to and watch polished singers or musicians play their instruments with poise, confidence, and unbridled joy. Using our musical metaphor theme, can you say that you play *your* song with poise, confidence, and joy? You may not even know what your song is.

I once asked a live audience this question at the conclusion of my speech: "If your life were a song today, what would the title be?" I meant for them to answer silently, but one gentleman quickly shouted out, "'Take This Job and Shove It"! While that certainly wasn't the answer I was hoping for, it definitely spoke to where he was in his life. As you might imagine, the audience went wild for his gut-wrenchingly honest answer! It's important to be honest with yourself when you're seeking to find your song. Let me ask you that same question: if your life were a song today, what would the title be?

What's the song in you? By the way, you're not limited to one. And your song will change over the different seasons of life. You may be a mom, but you're not *just* a mom. Don't be afraid to play all the notes and sing all the choruses. Let the record—oops, CD—oops, digital file play all the way to the end. If you listen to your whole song, it could be that you're a mom/great encourager/brilliant painter. Just as musical notes and instruments weave together to form complex and beautiful melodies, you too are a complex and beautiful symphony of possibility.

Perhaps you don't see yourself that way. What or who convinced you that you were something less than a fantastic and unique creation of God? King David took pause to study this very thought in Psalm 139:1–14. He sat down and penned this beautiful picture of God's concern, protection, and handiwork in our lives.

You have searched me, LORD, and you know me. You know when I sit and when I rise; you perceive my thoughts from afar. You discern my going out and my lying down; you are familiar with all my ways. Before a word is on my tongue you, LORD, know it completely. You hem me in behind and before, and you lay your hand upon me. Such knowledge is too wonderful for me, too lofty for me to attain. Where can I go from your Spirit? Where can I flee from your presence? If I go up to the heavens, you are there; if I make my bed in the depths, you are there. If I rise on the wings of the dawn, if I settle on the far side of the sea, even there your hand will guide me; your right hand will hold me fast. If I say, "Surely the darkness will hide me and the light become night around me," even the darkness will not be dark to you; the night will shine like the day, for darkness is as light to you. For you created my inmost being, you knit me together in my mother's womb. I praise you because I am fearfully and wonderfully made; your works are wonderful, I know that full well.

Do you know that *full well*, as David proclaimed? Can you believe that you were fearfully and wonderfully (and uniquely, I might add) made? Perhaps you, like so many, would like to believe that but find it difficult to see yourself that way. That's pretty common; sometimes this world can knock the confidence out of the most special people. Maybe you haven't heard this in a while, so let me tell you the truth: You're good. You've got talents and abilities that no one else has. You are truly special. You're wonderful. That's what the scripture says.

As you continue to pursue your own special song, I want you to know that I'm with you, and I believe God is as well. Even if *you* don't think you can do it, *I* do. I meet a lot of people, and I've never met anyone who didn't have unrealized potential. If you count yourself as a Christian believer, you may wish to consider that you are here for a reason.

In the apostle Paul's letter to the Romans, he said, "We know that in all things God works for the good of those who love him, who have been called according to his purpose" (8:28). What do you think? Have you been called for a purpose? Is there a song that burns in your heart that you're longing to sing? If so, that's a great place to start.

If you're passionate about something and willing to put in the effort to be good at it, you've begun to unlock the door to finding your song, your voice, and your purpose in life. We

talked about this earlier in the book, but let me ask again—
what do you love? Flowers, cooking, eating, writing, serving,
giving, helping, teaching, building—the sky really is the limit.
You are an integral piece of God's puzzle, and the picture isn't
complete without you. Your abilities, attitudes, and actions are
much needed in this world. You have a lifetime contract to play
in this league!

Again, the apostle Paul sums up this concept up so eloquently in his first letter to the Corinthians 12:12–27:

> Just as a body, though one, has many parts, but all its many
> parts form one body, so it is with Christ. For we were all baptized
> by one Spirit so as to form one body—whether Jews or Gentiles,
> slave or free—and we were all given the one Spirit to drink. Even
> so the body is not made up of one part but of many.
>
> Now if the foot should say, "Because I am not a hand, I do
> not belong to the body," it would not for that reason stop being
> part of the body. And if the ear should say, "Because I am not
> an eye, I do not belong to the body," it would not for that reason
> stop being part of the body. If the whole body were an eye, where
> would the sense of hearing be? If the whole body were an ear,
> where would the sense of smell be? But in fact God has placed
> the parts in the body, every one of them, just as he wanted them
> to be. If they were all one part, where would the body be? As it
> is, there are many parts, but one body.

The eye cannot say to the hand, "I don't need you!" And the head cannot say to the feet, "I don't need you!" On the contrary, those parts of the body that seem to be weaker are indispensable, and the parts that we think are less honorable we treat with special honor. And the parts that are unpresentable are treated with special modesty, while our presentable parts need no special treatment. But God has put the body together, giving greater honor to the parts that lacked it, so that there should be no division in the body, but that its parts should have equal concern for each other. If one part suffers, every part suffers with it; if one part is honored, every part rejoices with it. Now you are the body of Christ, and each one of you is a part of it.

Are you starting to get the message? You are more than a glob of cells that exists and then dies. You have a vital and essential role in life. It's good to be needed! You're needed. Of course, knowing this intellectually and truly feeling it in your heart are very different things. Our emotional, social, and spiritual self-perception is affected by our experiences. Perhaps you've been the recipient of an extra-large dosing of other people's comments and advice. The truth is that opinions are like noses—everyone has one and some are more "gifted" in this area than others.

To a certain degree, we're all concerned about what other people think of us. That's why you brushed your teeth this morning. However, as we mature we begin to discover what psychiatrist Daniel Amen, of PBS-TV fame, likes to call the 18/40/60 rule. When you're 18 you're terribly concerned about what other people think. When you're 40 you're not too concerned with what others think of you. When you're 60 you realize they weren't thinking about you at all—they were all thinking about themselves!

Still, other people's opinions of us can very much shape our thoughts, emotions, and actions, especially if they hold a position of importance in our lives—like a parent, coach, religious leader, teacher, spouse, or sibling. Our self-perception is affected, negatively or positively, by the input we receive from those who have influence in our lives, especially when we are young.

So, is who you perceive yourself to be defined by what other people think of you? It would be unusual if your answer was a flat no; we all see ourselves through others' eyes to some extent, but perhaps your life is *mostly* defined by what other people think of you. That's something to consider if you struggle with feelings of not being heard, seen, or valued enough. Perhaps you feel almost invisible, like you don't matter. Perhaps others have told you that's the real you—and you believed them.

Unfortunately, we can be so convinced by others' critical and inaccurate opinions that we begin to embrace them as our own. Whenever we face a challenge, we begin to hear the familiar voices in our heads telling us we can't do this, or we aren't good enough, or this will never work out. And as we embrace those negative opinions about ourselves, our actions begin to train other people how to treat us. It's like a self-fulfilling prophecy. How you perceive yourself affects how others perceive and treat you. If you perceive yourself as competent, worthy, lovable, and as someone who matters, others will, for the most part, see you and treat you that way.

But what if you view yourself as defective, unworthy, unlovable, weak, and less than? For a moment, rather than focus on what *other people* think of you and what *you* think of you, let's take a look at what *God* thinks of you. If God is real and Scripture is true, then God's perception of who you are may be very different from what your own perception is.

One thing for sure, *you must be of great value.* God made a sacrifice that none of us would make. He gave his Son in our place: "For God so loved the world that he gave his only begotten Son, that whoever believes in him shall not perish but have eternal life" (John 3:16 NASB). God gave his Son—you *must* be of great value.

Another thing is *God totally loves, wants, and accepts you—* just like you are right now. Scripture says you can come to God just as you are, with no judgment or condemnation. John 3:17

says, "For God did not send his Son into the world to condemn the world, but to save the world through him," and Romans 8:1 says, "Therefore, there is now no condemnation for those who are in Christ Jesus."

No condemnation and *full* acceptance. You may have been longing for this all of your life. Perhaps you can hardly imagine what it would be like to live a life with no condemnation and loving, unconditional acceptance. Perhaps your life is filled with condemning, accusing inner voices that challenge your worth. And perhaps the loudest voice comes from *you*. You don't like yourself and treat yourself accordingly. You wouldn't be friends with someone who treated you as badly as you treat yourself. If this sounds like you, I'd like to introduce you to the concept of grace.

Scripture is filled with comments about God's grace toward us. In the scriptural context, grace is best described as *unmerited favor*. You can't earn it, may not deserve it, and can't buy it. It's given freely—you don't even have to ask, it's just there.

Wait a minute, you may be thinking. *Are you saying that God wants to help me, with no strings attached; all I have to do is accept his help?* That's what the Scriptures say. Ephesians 2:8 says, "For it is by grace you have been saved, through faith—and this is not from yourselves, it is the *gift* of God" (my emphasis). So if you believe Scripture is true, take the gift.

That may be hard to hear—that you are special. You matter. You are lovable and deeply, genuinely loved. It's not just me saying that—Scripture says that. You may be thinking, *But you don't know what I've done. God could never accept me.* It's true, we all have a public and private life, and only God knows what goes on in private. But if you're hearing the voice in your head playing the *I'm not good enough, I don't measure up* message, hear this as well: people who say they don't have problems are *liars.* In 1 John 1:8, it says, "If we say that we have no sin, we are deceiving ourselves and the truth is not in us (NASB)." God knows you have good and bad parts—and, as we've discussed, the bad does not negate the good; they simply coexist.

God's acceptance of us is not based on how good we are! Remember, Romans 3:23 says, "we *all* have sinned and fall short of God's glory" (my emphasis). I'm telling you the truth—unless you struggle with genuine narcissistic personality disorder (very rare), you don't know how good, valuable, and loved you really are! You can't even imagine how much God loves you!

Yes, you have good parts and bad parts. Yes, you'll have seasons of ups and downs in your life. Yes, you will be hurt and you'll make mistakes. But hold on to this—you never, ever have to worry about this one thing: *God loves you.* God has seen everything that has ever happened in your life and accepts you right now, right here, just as you are. Can you hear that?

God loves you right now, right here, just as you are. If you're going to find your song and embrace your passions and purpose, it will help you to get that settled in your mind and spirit.

So much for God—what about you? How do *you* feel about you? As we covered earlier in this chapter, how you perceive yourself affects how others perceive and treat you. In truth, even the most "beautiful" people are rarely satisfied with the way they look and feel. If Hollywood stars can't be pleased with themselves, what chance do the rest of us have? I think the trap for many people is that very often their sense of personhood comes from the outside, not from the inside. If you, in your deepest inner being, know the truth about who you are and what you're worth, no one can convince you of a lie.

Let's consider the path to finding your personal song and singing it with delight and intention. Using the word *song* as our acronym, here are some basic thoughts:

<u>S</u>ee things for what they are, *not* what you'd like them to be or what they used to be. Whatever is happening now, whoever you are right now, wherever you find yourself—embrace it! Notice I didn't say *accept* it; I said *embrace* it. Embracing your life for what it is, and yourself for who you are, is a proactive stance that moves you to do what you can with what you have. You'll likely be surprised by just how much you really *can* do if you give your life and yourself a giant hug.

<u>O</u>pen the door for possibility. As you begin to move forward in discovering your life's passions and meaning, you'll find you make more progress if you don't place the roadblocks of doubt in the way. You may not succeed in everything you try, but you will not always fail either. Stop playing the movie forward in your head and trying to predict the outcome. You really don't know what's going to happen until you try. Both Matthew and Mark's gospels record the words of Jesus proclaiming that with God on your side, "all things are possible."

<u>N</u>ever give up. Quoting again from American baseball icon and philosopher Yogi Berra: "It ain't over till it's over!" As we've discussed, your life on earth is finite. It had a beginning and will someday have an end. Of course, as Christians we believe the end of this life is simply the beginning of an eternal life, a life in which the cares of our earthly existence will quickly fade. Until that day you have a mission for which you are uniquely equipped by your ability and experience. In the book of Acts 20:24, the apostle Paul is quoted as saying, "My only aim is to finish the race and complete the task the Lord Jesus has given me." It's always too soon to quit.

<u>G</u>et help. While you are uniquely qualified to sing your song, you'll sound better with a band and backup singers. We all need help; it is not a sign of weakness or failure. Rather, acknowledging that you need help from time to time is a healthy embrace of reality. Even the Lone Ranger had Tonto. A life that pursues too much solitude is a life poorly spent.

Remember, finding and singing your song in life is not just about you. Like it or not, everything you do affects someone else. Hitting your stride and finding your "sweet spot" will make you an effective influencer and, in fact, a world changer. You may not change the whole world, like some of history's heroes we've discussed, but you may very well change *someone's* whole world. When you're operating within the confidence and power of your gifts and heartfelt desires, your life can *literally* give life to others.

Your life means the world to someone—maybe someone you've not even met. You'll never know what *is* possible unless you start to sing your song. Just start with the first note and the rest will come. One thing for sure, you'll never find meaning in your life until you begin to pursue it. Watching the game from the sidelines is not the same as playing in it. Just do what's in front of you and take the first step—you have nothing to lose and everything to gain!

Let's close by returning to our solfège musical theme: do, re, mi, fa, sol, la, ti, do.

Do: Do the right thing. Call it our conscience, our brain's prefrontal cortex activity, or Pinocchio's Jiminy Cricket. Most of us have an innate sense of right and wrong. When your values are clear, when you know your personal song by heart, decisions are easy. You never go wrong by doing the right thing.

Re: Realize your potential. I don't care who you are or what you've done; you are a bundle of unrealized potential. Every season of your life offers opportunities to learn, grow, and fulfill your ultimate purpose. Don't waste another minute.

Mi: Mind your manners. Sometimes it's not as much what you do as how you do it. Navigating your life in the context of grace and kindness will serve you and those around you better. Taking "the high road" is a better path to peace and fulfillment.

Fa: Failures can become fertilizer. In this success-driven world, we sometimes forget that the road to every success is invariably paved with potholes of failure. Knowing what doesn't work is just as important as knowing what does. Failure is only a deal breaker if you quit trying.

So: Solutions begin with me. Draw a small circle around your feet. You have now successfully identified the one thing in life you have control over. You cannot control others' actions, thoughts, and behaviors. Attempting to do so will break your heart and spirit. Doing what you can, owning your part, is essential to making your "life song" truly yours.

La: Laugh. Life is short. Really, it is. If you're not having any fun, something is out of balance. Pursuing activities and relationships that bring you joy is an integral part of discovering your best life. I seriously doubt anyone ever whispered with their last breath, "I wish I'd frowned more."

Ti: Time is valuable; use it wisely. In many years of speaking and singing, I've come to really appreciate the time I spend with my audiences. What used to feel like a performance now feels like a gift. I'm reminded of the show-business adage, "When you take someone's money, you just take their money. But when you take their time, you take a piece of their life." As you've taken the time to read this book, you've honored me with a piece of your life—I'm so very grateful! Thank you! Whom have *you* shared a piece of your life with today? Wisely spending your most valuable asset, your time, is an investment that pays great dividends. You can measure your return in the relationships you build and the legacy you leave.

Do: We're back to doing the right thing. Certainly some things are right for everyone—universal truths that help us move toward health, hope, and healing in this sometimes difficult world. However, beyond the obvious sameness we all share, there is magnificent uniqueness in you. If you hear little else from this book, I want you to hear this: You are special. Do the right thing and redeem your time; make the most of it. That may sound a bit crazy coming from a lady who almost took her own life a few years ago, but I have discovered the precious value of life.

You matter. Your life was not an accident, and your future is not set in stone. As I travel the country speaking to corporate, convention, and faith-based groups, I've learned that everyone has a story—no one gets through life without struggle. No matter what you've been through, or are going through right now, things can change. The good, the bad, and the in-between—it's all been preparation for this very moment in your life.

No one who has ever lived has had the same life experiences as you. No one who has ever lived has the biological, psychological, and spiritual construction you possess. When God made you, he broke the mold. Your "song" has been written over the course of your lifetime, and it's a glorious work in progress. Are you ready? Clear your throat and begin to walk onto your "stage." Perhaps your current stage is shuttling the kids to school, designing skyscrapers, feeding the poor, or being a great and supportive friend; maybe it's all those things and much, much more.

Maestro, if you please. The reader of this book has a great and magnificent song to sing. It's a song that has been written with joy and tears over the course of a lifetime . . . a song only they can sing well. Instruct the orchestra to prepare for something wonderful and distinctive—you have never heard anything like it, ever.

Reader, are you ready to sing? You're on!

ACKNOWLEDGMENTS

LaDonna:

There are so many people to thank for making this book a reality . . . where do I begin?

First, I want to thank my husband and best friend, Tim Johnson, for being the "rock" in my life. If it weren't for him, I would have never had the courage to "find my voice and sing my own song" thirty-plus years ago.

To my children and grandchildren . . . you are a never-ending source of absolute delight to me.

I'm grateful to have been born into the Gatlin Family. I've learned so much about life by sharing the stage with my brothers Larry, Steve, and Rudy. And I'm forever grateful for the never-ending support of our parents. Bless you, Mom and Dad!

Thank you, Dr. Todd Clements, for introducing me to my coauthor, Dr. Mike Marino, without whom this book would never have been written . . . literally. Mike's insights, expertise, and wealth of experience make the text "sing"!

Thanks, Michael Harriot, for finding this book a good home with the folks at HCI. And thank you, HCI, for making me feel at home. Candace Johnson, you dot every "i" and cross every "t" . . . literally and figuratively!

Finally . . . and most importantly . . . thank God for His divine providence in my life.

Proverbs 3:5–6: "Trust in the LORD with all your heart and lean not on your own understanding; in all your ways acknowledge him, and He will make your paths straight."

Mike:

My heartfelt thanks to LaDonna for being so transparent in telling her story and to my friend Todd Clements, MD, for introducing us. Much thanks also to Candace Johnson and the HCI publishing family for embracing this book with such zeal.

To my agent, Michael Harriot, kudos for going the extra mile, and to God's three greatest gifts to me—Mallory, Joey, and Marisa, thanks for being the inspiration for every good thought and work in my life.

ABOUT
THE AUTHORS

L aDonna Gatlin, CSP, CPAE, is the sister of the legendary Gatlin Brothers and a National Speaker Association Hall of Famer. She brings her "family over fame" story to hundreds of thousands of people as an active member of the National Speakers Association and has earned its highest professional designation, the Certified Speaking Professional (CSP). In July of 2005, LaDonna was one of five speakers (and the only woman that year) inducted into the

Speakers Hall of Fame (CPAE Council of Peers Award for Excellence), a lifetime award for speaking excellence and professionalism.

LaDonna has spent her entire career empowering people to "sing their own song" through their words, deeds, and actions. A seasoned professional, LaDonna has shared her message everywhere . . . from corporate powerhouses to the prison cells of death row. She truly speaks from the heart with stories that are the stuff of life, driving home common sense wisdom for everyday living in the process. Her presentations educate, inspire, and entertain and are an unforgettable experience for her audiences.

In addition to her live presentations, LaDonna has also recorded four solo CDs and is a contributing writer to the bestselling book series Chicken Soup for the Soul. LaDonna lives in a Dallas suburb with her husband (and best friend!) of thirty-seven years, Tim Johnson. They have two adult children who have blessed them with five grandchildren. For more information, please visit www.ladonnagatlin.com.

Mike Marino, PhD, is a speaker, author, counselor, and media personality with an extensive background in mental healthcare and communications. He hosted a nationally syndicated call-in radio program for five years and has produced broadcast programming, live events, and written materials for such diverse people as Dr. Laura Schlessinger, PBS-TV's Daniel Amen, MD, and the Reverend Billy Graham. He has also served as corporate vice president at the world renowned Amen Clinics, as president of New Life Ministries, where he presided over a nationwide network of over 600 mental health clinicians, and as a senior executive at the Billy Graham Evangelistic Association. His hands-on, practical experience running psychiatric hospitals and substance abuse recovery centers has laid the groundwork for his life-changing message of genuine hope and healing.

To learn more, please visit www.TheADbootcamp.com.

"Princess" at age one

Induction into the Hall of Fame at the National Speakers Association Convention, 2005

The Gatlin Quartet, 1960

Backstage in Branson, Missouri, at the Gatlin Brothers Christmas Show, 2006

LaDonna and Tim Johnson, December 21, 1974

Johnson family, 2011

Gatlin siblings celebrate Mom and Dad's 65th wedding anniversary, 2011